HERE IN HOPE: A NATURAL HISTORY

Hope from Mount Hope. Coquihalla River to the right; Fraser River at the top, just before it changes direction. Note the flare to the Fraser River Bridge at left, and the angled streets that originally paralleled the Kettle Valley Railroad tracks as they crossed the delta from the bridge over the Coquihalla to the bridge over the Fraser.

HERE IN HOPE

A NATURAL HISTORY

J. M. BRIDGEMAN

OOLICHAN BOOKS

LANTZVILLE, BRITISH COLUMBIA, CANADA

2002

Canadian Cataloguing in Publication Data

Main entry under title:
Bridgeman, Joan, 1948-
Here in Hope

Includes bibliographical references.
ISBN 0-88982-212-3

1. Hope (B.C.)—History. I. Title.
FC3849.H66B74 2002 971.1'37 C2002-910139-5
F1089.5.H66B74 2002

The Canada Council | Le Conseil des Arts
for the Arts | du Canada

We gratefully acknowledge the support of the Canada Council for the Arts for our publishing program.

BRITISH
COLUMBIA
ARTS COUNCIL
Supported by the Province of British Columbia

Grateful acknowledgement is also made to the BC Ministry of Tourism, Small Business and Culture for their financial support.

We acknowledge the financial support of the Government of Canada through the Book Publishing Industry Development Program for our publishing activities.

Published by
Oolichan Books
P.O. Box 10, Lantzville
British Columbia, Canada
V0R 2H0

Printed in Canada

Acknowledgements

This book would not have been possible without the help of many people. Sincere thanks to: the geologists—Dan Cardinal, John Clague, J. M. Journeay, and Dr. Leith of the University of Manitoba; any errors reflect my amateur's understanding. Thanks also to: the photographers—John Riley, Wilderness Therapy; Rick Easterbrook, Perceptions; Jenny Wolpert; and the British Columbia Archives, Visual Records section. Thanks to the readers—Jack Delair, Jeff Long, Barry Stewart, Jim Tallosi; to Clancy Wolpert and the Hope Outdoors Club; to friends in the Hope Writers Guild, including Irene Bjerky, Marilyn Meden, Molly Rychter, and Fran Martin who explained that "the mountains are my church"; and to the Hope and District Historical Society for their groundbreaking publication, *Forging a New Hope: Struggles and Dreams 1848-1948: A Pioneer Story of Hope, Flood, and Laidlaw*. Thanks also to others who fed me information, books, or encouragement, including Laura Addinall, Tim Bowling, Judy Brown, Pam Delmas, Carol Hurst, Carol Nelson, Lawrence Hope, John Nihei, Jeff Such, Lindsay Thacker, Ron Smith of Oolichan, and my editor, Hiro Boga.

Thanks to the Fraser Valley Regional District for permission to use part of their map, and to Shannon Sigurdson for his technical assistance.

Every effort has been made to secure clearance to quote previously published materials used in this book. If you can supply missing copyright information, please contact the publisher.

I am grateful for the assistance of the Hudson's Bay Company Archives, the Provincial Archives of Manitoba, for use of quotations from the George Simpson Dispatches and for the Fort Hope file.

Front Cover—Coquihalla Granite. Photo: John Riley, Wilderness Therapy. Weathered granite with Indian Paintbrush (red flower) and Arnica (yellow flower).

Contents

MAP

DISTRICT OF HOPE

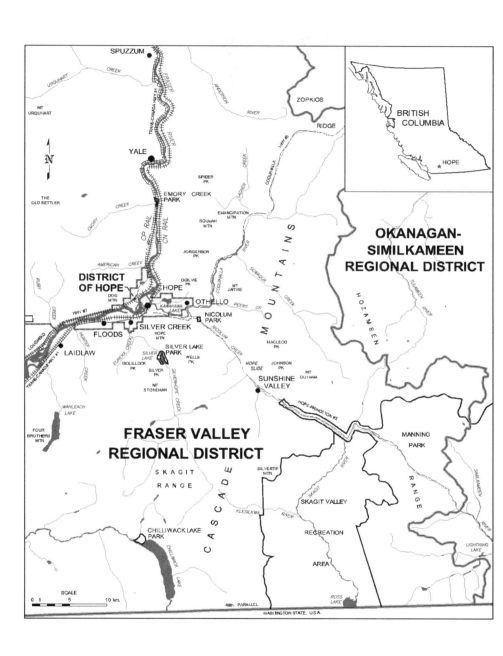

THE FRIENDSHIP GARDEN

"Mountains and Waters are a dyad that together make wholeness possible. . . . The compound 'mountains and waters'—*shan-shui* in Chinese—is the straightforward term for landscape."

—Gary Snyder,
"Blue Mountains Constantly Walking"
from *The Practice of the Wild.*

" . . . smooth stones from the brook of time,
worn round by constant friction of tongues
long silent."

—Andrew Lang

The Friendship Garden

Approach it from any of several directions, this garden of rock and water and trees. Pebblestone benches await visitors. A grey lantern, a miniature curve-roofed shrine, stands in the pond here in this quiet centre of Hope. Downtown Hope, in beautiful British Columbia. The falling water, the receptive pool, the tumbled medley of boulders and verdure stop the breath with their beauty.

This Japanese Friendship Garden, bringing East and West together, interpreting oriental traditions with local native materials, was a gift to the people of Hope. During World War II, the province of British Columbia pressured the federal government to invoke the War Measures Act. Canadians of Japanese heritage were forced to move at least one hundred miles from the seacoast. Some were interned at Tashme, twenty kilometres east of here, on what is now the Hope-Princeton Highway. Their homes, automobiles, fishing boats, and businesses at the Coast were confiscated and sold. After the war, when the camps were finally closed and the gates to Hope were unlocked, some of those detained at Tashme chose to settle here and become a part of the community. Forty years later, the Canadian government made a token cash redress to internees and their descendants. In 1991, some citizens of Japanese heritage designed and built this garden honouring the internees and gave it to the town as a symbol of friendship and unity.

The plantings, the lantern, the manmade rockfall, the water cascading into the pool, all calm the spirit. The subtle ordering seduces the eye, creates focus, highlights the beauty of the ordinary. Follow the curve of the granite boulders, up, over the encircling trees, to the natural surround in which this garden and town are set. The rocks, hills, and mountains of Hope. What else do they remember? What other stories do these stones have to tell?

PLANET EARTH

"From space . . . Earth is . . .
a single interactive sphere of life,
a living organism composed of air, water and earth, fragile,
as Dr. Musgrave says, floating in the velvet void of space . . ."

—Wade Davis, "The End of the Wild"
from *The Clouded Leopard:
Travels to Landscapes of Spirit and Desire.*

PLANET EARTH

On a map of the Earth, Hope sits 23' north of the forty-ninth parallel of latitude, 26' 20" west of the 121st meridian of longitude, far from the Greenwich mean, near the United States. With these readings, we humans attempt to locate ourselves on the page, in the larger picture, to mark our place so that others may find us. However, the stories the rocks of Hope have to tell pre-date human history by millions of years. The story of Hope is part of the story of the Earth itself, its geology, its geomorphology, its orogeny. The story of Hope is part of the story of the North American continent, the growth of its cordilleran backbone, the tracing and erasing of successive periods of glaciation, the arrival of its human populations. The story of Hope is part of the political history of Europe, of Great Britain and British North America, of the United States, and of Canada. The story of Hope is part of the history of the province of British Columbia, its evolution from ancestral land to disputed territory to colony to province, its on-going role in the continued migration of humans moving over the spinning globe.

Dreams of riches, dreams of freedom, of a fresh start on a clean slate, inspire people to move. To travel far from home, to create a community, to craft a meaningful and fulfilling life in a new land requires hope. When we let go of the false security of concrete and crowds, the mountains and waters of Hope, like all wild places, remind us that mankind did not create this world, is neither maker nor master. For millennia before the arrival of human beings, mountains rose, snow fell, water trickled to a flow. The rocks whisper that we humans are an afterthought, a late arrival in this paradise of beauty and wonder. Created out of the Earth itself, we are dreamed by her, spun, recycled from the same molecules, from the very dust we eat and breathe. Moving mountains rush through the watershed of our bodies in the eternal flux of growth and change.

In the beginning, science theorizes, perhaps six billion years ago, Earth was a spinning ball of gases. As its temperature changed, different elements and compounds separated out, each melting or solidifying at its own specific point on an imaginary thermometer. The sphere transformed over time from gas to viscous liquid to solid, becoming the planet we know today—a mass of hot magma at the core, surrounded by a mantle of rocks with the least dense closest to the surface, and covered by a crust, a hardened thin skin. Convection and pressures from above and from below caused the crust to stretch and eventually to split or crack into segments called plates that float atop the mantle.

The movement of plates, up and down, over, under or into each other, is called plate tectonics. Plate tectonics is a relatively recent theory (barely thirty years old) which explains many previously mysterious geologic observations. Over spans of hundreds of millions of years, the theory suggests, the Earth's crust separated into continental and oceanic plates. The continental plate split apart into the shapes roughly corresponding to the continents as we know them today. South America separated from Africa; North America drifted west from Europe.

The original western edge of the North American continental plate (ancestral North America) reached only as far as today's Rocky Mountains. Calgary, eight hundred kilometres northeast from Hope, and Pincher Creek, eight hundred kilometres straight east, would have had ocean views. The western continental shelf, layers of sediment built up underwater from deposits dropped by freshwater rivers flowing into the ocean, extended some five hundred kilometres, to about Salmon Arm, three hundred kilometres northeast of Hope. So on a map of the Earth for two hundred million years ago, British Columbia west of the Rockies does not exist. There is no place called Hope. Longitude 121 West crosses ocean. Moreover, even in pre-history, the western edge of this continent was younger, and was pushing out from, building up from the east.

NEW
LAND
FORMATION

"The blue mountains march out of the sea,
shoulder the sky for a while,
and slip back into the waters."

—Gary Snyder,
"Blue Mountains Constantly Walking"
from *The Practice of the Wild.*

New Land Formation

Southwestern British Columbia is a collage of fragments of the Earth's crust brought together over time. Geologists are still working at explaining the process, at deconstructing the creation of this collage. The story begins in the east, along the provincial boundary. The lower half of the British Columbia-Alberta border today runs along the extremity of ancestral North America. The rugged Rocky Mountains delineate this old edge. On a map, this line, angling at almost forty-five degrees like a backslash \ , is said to be northwest trending. The Rockies are the beginning of the *cordillera,* a Spanish word meaning "a little string or line." The mountains run like a cord or a spine down the back of the continent.

Looking nothing like a gentle shoreline, the Rockies today rise high above the plains to their east. Their jagged crags, above the snowline all year round, were raised by physical processes. Convection, movement from warm into cool, and rifting, the spreading apart of the ocean floor as new matter pushes up through mid-oceanic ridges, created currents that thrust the eastern edge of the oceanic plate slowly toward the continental plate. When the oceanic plate landed (touched the edge of the continent) and subducted (jammed underneath), it raised the continental plate, lifting it up thousands of metres. The uplifted sediments were left above water level, visible. Wind, water, and ice eroded the exposed layers of seacoast into alpine land formations—the horns, cirques, aretes, cols, and tarns of the Rocky Mountain landscape we see today. Under the right conditions, with a light dusting of snow, the original horizontal layers or strata of the sediments are still evident.

Movement of the oceanic plate also folded the underwater sediments along the old continental shelf the way a loose rug pushes up into ripples when you slide into it. These folds and ripples too were lifted above sea level. The new land along the old edge of ancestral North America formed waves of mountain ranges that run parallel to the old coastline, repeating the northwest-trending angle of the Alberta-British Columbia border. Growing for fifty million years, the mineral-rich Columbia Mountains (the Selkirks, Purcells, and Monashees east of the Okanagan Valley) extended the continent westward from the Rockies by 150 million years ago.

Intense pressure along the edges where plates met also caused huge chunks (terranes) to twist or break off. A terrane may have been a part of a continental plate or a part of an oceanic plate. After terranes broke off the main plate, they travelled on their own, typically in the same northwest-trending direction as the mountains, because the oceanic plate continued to push inland, east, from the south. Part of a terrane may have landed on top of another terrane and stayed. Part of a terrane may have landed on top of another only to be uplifted or folded or flipped later. Much of the story of terranes is still a complex mystery with a difficult-to-follow, distorted time line.

So new land formed west of ancestral North America by rising from the ocean floor, by the rippling and folding of sediments at the continent's edge, by being uplifted, and by breaking off and attaching elsewhere. Where plates collided, the oceanic plate continued to push down and under and the lighter continental plate slipped over top. Along the line where the oceanic plate subducted, a trench swallowed material pushed into it from the west. Sometimes this material was melted and recycled, digested and disgorged. Sometimes it retained its original form and reappeared later during an uplift.

Another way that new land was created was by the intrusion of molten magma from the earth's mantle to near the surface, under the crust, or by the extrusion of magma above the surface. The subduction zone between two plates provides an opening where molten material from the mantle can force or intrude its way up. Volcanic extrusions of lava bubble up through openings and spread out in flow or shield volcanoes or build up as conical-shaped mountains. Alternatively, plutonic intrusions, often molten granite or basalt rock composed of a mixture of minerals, well up like lumpy bread dough rising. The molten rock cools and solidifies below the surface. The crust above plutonic intrusions eventually erodes away, exposing plutons or batholiths, a pluton that covers more than one hundred square kilometres. Then the new granite or basalt rock is pushed and scrunched by the eastward creeping oceanic plate, creating waves of rock, ridge crests, a sea of mountain ranges forming a new West Coast.

It is during periods of igneous activity, volcanism, that precious metals, crystals, and indicator minerals melt and cool. At certain predictable temperatures, gold, silver, copper, lead, zinc, nickel, or iron melts from the matrix and flows into spaces in other rock. As the melted material cools, it solidifies as a nugget, vein, or dyke. Also, at their own specific temperatures, diamonds, rubies, garnets imbedded in a matrix crystallize. As molten rocks cool slowly, large granular crystals grow with time. Rapid cooling causes molten rock to solidify in minute grains barely visible to the naked eye. Indicator minerals such as veins of quartz or serpentine solidify near or intrude into other deposits.

The process of new land formation continued. Sediments from the Columbia Mountains landmass were deposited over its new western edge into the Okanagan Trough. The oceanic plate continued to push in from the west, rippling, uplifting. Terranes pulled away and left, exposing bedrock outcrops like those seen along Lake Okanagan. More sediments were deposited; more magma intruded and extruded; metals melted and cooled. For one hundred million years, the Cascade Mountains grew along this western side of the North American continental plate. Land for Hope was created by fifty to forty million years ago.

Running from northern California to Kamloops, from Osoyoos to Hope, the Cascade Mountains display an exhilarating diversity of rock and mountain-forming activity—sedimentary, metamorphic, and igneous (volcanic and plutonic). The Cascades developed in three main surges that are identified as separate mountain ranges. Farthest east and oldest, the Okanagan Range extends north to about Keremeos. The Hozameen Range extends west and north to Lytton and south of Manning Park into Washington State. Sediments from this range were deposited along its western edge. As new land formation continued, these sediments were uplifted to form the Hozameen Ridge, sharp-peaked sedimentary mountains that once marked the edge of the continent. In Hope, Mount Ogilvie and Thacker Mountain below it are mountains composed of metamorphosed sedimentary rock which was once underwater before being pushed upward and then eroded. Oceanic marine fossils have been found on Mount Ogilvie and a fold in the sedimentary layers is clearly visible near the switchback on Thacker Mountain Road.

However, the Cascades did not stop with the Hozameen Range; they continued to grow. Plate tectonics pushed the Hozameen in and up. Older rock continued to erode. Water deposited sediments along the ocean edge, carving stream channels and river courses. Magma from the mantle intruded below the surface and extruded as lava above the surface. The Skagit Range, the third in the Cascades, is the youngest. The northern tip of the Skagit Range ends here, at Mount Hope. The Skagit Range curves towards the west. Its uplifted ridge, with hanging waterfalls that were once streams entering the ocean, can be seen clearly behind Mount Cheam, ringing the Upper Fraser Valley east and south of Chilliwack. Thus, Hope straddles the line where two Cascade ranges meet. The Coquihalla River, running between Mount Ogilvie, part of the Hozameen Range, and Mount Hope, in the Skagit Range, created the delta upon which the old town of Hope sits. The Fraser River, crashing into the northern tip of the Skagit Range's hard igneous rock makes an abrupt right turn here at the Hope waterfront.

Eastward from Hope, the Cascades, called historically the Hope Mountains, provide the topographic challenge. The old Hudson's Bay Company Brigade Trails, the Kettle Valley Railway, and the Coquihalla Highway all cross the Hozameen Range. The Dewdney Trail and the Hope-Princeton Highway start out from Hope up the valley between the Hozameen and Skagit ranges.

In the Friendship Garden, the quiet centre of unity, where water falls into a pool ringed by greenery, the rocks were gathered from several different areas in the district. The grey granite boulders were acquired from a highway construction site near Flood and are thus part of the Skagit Range of the Cascade Mountains. The pointed peak behind the garden, Mount Ogilvie, that rises above the town like an arrowhead at the tip of Wallace Street, is part of the Hozameen Range. Its picture-postcard view is no accident. As the highest elevation, the Royal Engineers used it as a landmark when they first surveyed the townsite. To the First Nations, this peak was *quem-quema*, meaning "many-breasts." The Royal Engineers re-named the mountain for the Hudson's Bay Company clerk John D. B. Ogilvy who climbed up and planted the Union Jack atop its peak on Queen Victoria's fortieth birthday in 1859.

In water-formed mountains like Mount Ogilvie, sediments from the continent were deposited in distinct layers in the ocean and then compressed into sedimentary rock—sand into sandstone, mud into shale, clay into slate. Then forces such as deep burial and heating changed the rocks. Silica deposits metamorphosed into chert; sandstone emerged as quartzite; limestone, calcite or dolomite transformed into marble; shale became schist. Fire-formed igneous rock, molten lava, extruded at the Earth's surface or intruded below the surface or popped up between concordant sections of country rock, interfering with the old sediments. Horizontal layers were curved or bent. Before, during, or after all this excitement, the oceanic plate pushed ever in and uplifted the old continental edge. This orogeny accounts for the incredible variety of rock formations around Hope. This is a region of geologic turmoil, a place of transition, where things end and new things begin. We who dwell here literally live on edges, straddling from one range to another as we go about our daily tasks.

The highest peak in the Canadian Cascades is in the Okanagan Range—Lakeview Mountain (2628 metres) in Cathedral Provincial Park east of Manning Park. Spread out beyond the Manning Park Lookout, jagged Cascade peaks scratch the sky: Chuwanten (2148 m), Windy Joe (1825 m), Frosty (2408 m), Lone Goat (2004 m), Red Mountain (2022 m), the Hozameen Ridge, and the Skagit Range.

Mountains and waters together create a landscape. Highway #3 coming west through the Allison Pass (1341 m) crosses the Skagit River seven times before it climbs the spectacular Skagit Bluffs high above the valley floor. On its way into Hope, it rounds Mount Outram (2452 m) and passes the rubble that fell from Johnson Ridge. The rockfall visible at the Hope Slide Lookout is part of the ridge of the Hozameen Range. When it fell into the valley of Nicolum Creek, which now runs west between the Hozameen and the Skagit ranges towards the Coquihalla and Fraser rivers and thence into Georgia Strait, it divided the waters from their upstream sources. A few kilometres east of the Slide, water runs south and west via the Skagit River into Puget Sound. Thirty or forty kilometres east of the Slide, the waters of Lightning Lake in Manning Park flow north and east into the Similkameen and Okanagan rivers, part of the Columbia River watershed. The clandestine routes the waters trace record undocumented stories of creation and land formation. Although national and provincial borders frequently follow parallels and meridians, local geographic boundaries often correspond to watersheds. Summits in mountainous regions divide the waters; borderlines are drawn from peak to peak.

The Coquihalla Highway (#5) traverses the Hozameen Range. Following the Coquihalla River north, the highway crosses the Plutonic Belt of the Hozameens at Zopkios Ridge (1800 m), the Coquihalla Pass summit, skirting the Needle and granite peaks named as recently as the 1970s after alpine ruminants—Alpaca, Vicuna, Yak, Nak, Chamois, Llama, Gemse, Serna, Bighorn, Guanaco. Hozameen peaks visible from Hope include Mount Ogilvie (1615 m), Jarvis, and Macleod Peak. Up the Fraser Canyon on the Trans-Canada Highway (#1), the peaks to the right, across the river—Jorgenson, Squeah, Emancipation, and Spider—are the Hozameen Ridge of the old Cascade edge.

On the other side of the Fraser River, back from the road, Old Settler (2145 m), Urquhart (2100 m), and Skuzzy (2217 m) are part of the Coast Mountains. New land formation did not stop at Hope. Deposition, folding, uplift, intrusion, extrusion, and erosion continued; over the last fifty million years, a whole new series of mountains rose along this still-growing West Coast. On the Fraser River's north shore, the Lougheed Highway (#7) crosses the southernmost slopes of the Coast Mountains. Thus the Fraser River in Hope marks yet another edge—the boundary between the Cascade Mountains to the east and south, and the Coast Mountains to the west and north.

In the Cascade Mountains, peaks of the Skagit Range visible from Hope include Mount Hope (1849 m), Silver Peak, Mount Isolillock (Holy Cross, 2088 m), and Eureka Peak. Up Silverhope Creek, from Silver-Skagit Road, you see the backside of Mount Hope and Wells Peak, Stoneman, Silvertip (2250 m), and Shawatum (2158 m). At Ross Lake, Hozomeen Peak (2459 m; note the American spelling) looms over the International Boundary, with Desolation (1860 m) standing behind. Visible from Mount Outram east of Hope, Washington State's 3285 metre (10,800 foot) snow-tipped volcanic cone, Mount Baker, is some eighty kilometres to the south and west, accessed by road through Sumas, off #1, past Cheam (2107 m), Slesse (2424 m), Liumchen and other Cascade peaks above the piedmont overlooking the Fraser Valley floor and the freeway.

Draw out these curling ribbons of blue, gold, and silver rivers, these swirling threads of grey and gravel roads, of green trails. Weave them under and over where they meet and cross each other. Gather, twirl them into a rosette. Knot them into a tassel and dangle it over the garden at the centre of town where everything comes together. Hope straddles the old edges that meet here. The rivers run between Hozameen and Skagit Ranges, between the Cascade and Coast Mountains. Yet, it is to the Cascades that Hope relates. Residents monitor the snowline, the bare patch on Mount Hope, or the white symbol on Holy Cross. Oriented to the peak of Mount Ogilvie, downtown bathes in the shine of moonlight off Macleod's snow-capped tip.

Hope guards the secret locations of trailheads, those portals into the wild. At the confluence of the rivers. At the end of Thacker Mountain Road. Along Thacker Marsh. From the end of Kettle Valley Road, on the abandoned railbed into the Coquihalla Canyon. Up Mount Hope at Exit 170, or up its backside, on the four-wheel drive road off #3 that winds to decommissioned logging roads or to trails over the top. From the end of the weigh station parking lot on #7, across the railroad tracks over to Landstrom Ridge. Off Exit 165, a short pilgrimage in to Flood Falls. Sole to ground, hikers entering cathedral-like second growth step into the play of light flickering through the green canopy, wade into the pool, breathe in the mist of melted ice rock falling from eroded granite tiers.

From the Cascades, waters emerge clean. The Hope Mountains define Hope. Skagit ramparts guard our secrets; the Hozameen inform our dreams.

ON THE EDGE

"Where the mountain pass is narrow,
and the torrent white and strong."

—E. Pauline Johnson, "The Trail to Lillooet"
from *Flint and Feather.*

On the Edge

West of the Friendship Garden, Landstrom Ridge (also called Crack Mountain), an igneous intrusion, sits where the Fraser River begins the S-curve that changes its direction here at Hope. The Landstrom Ridge trailhead is accessed across the railroad tracks from the end of the weigh station parking lot along #7 highway. The trail is rudimentary, a narrow path slashed through the underbrush, conforming to the jagged elevations of the underlying rock. Yet from this footpath, views from the ridge in four directions are awe-inspiring. On a glorious spring day, the mosses and lichens are electric green. The Chocolate Lily, in speckled camouflage, hides in old and new grass.

At the first lookout, the V where the hills and cliffs meet river and sky points west towards Vancouver, 150 kilometres away. Highways #7 and #1, leading to and from the coast, line the valley along both sides of the river. The flat land along the south shore of the Fraser

River has been developed—old growth forest cleared to farms, a logging yard, an airstrip, a truck stop, and the streets and houses of Silver Creek and Flood, now part of the District of Hope. Before the freshet, sand deposited in swirls and bars along the riverbed is exposed like a tidewater flat at low ebb. Rockhounds comb the cobble for jade, gold, and agate.

The trail stops at the cliff edge. Hikers pause, shy back, silent with wonder. It may not hit them, like the slap of a wave on the face, there on top of the mountain, where moss burns in the sun. Perhaps later, the way consciousness wafts in after a dream, they realize that where they stood was once the edge of the continent, that what they gazed upon was not always there, that Landstrom Ridge was at one time the land's end. Fifty million years ago, there was nothing between Hope and the ocean. Before the Coast Mountains were created, the Cascades marked the western edge of the North American continent.

Forty million years ago, the curved line of the Cascades swept from California to Kamloops through what is now downtown Hope. Today, the Fraser River north to Lytton, running as it does here between the Cascade and the Coast Mountains, outlines that old edge. The headwaters of the Fraser rise in the Rocky Mountains near Jasper National Park, some eleven hundred metres above sea level. The water rushes northwest through the Rocky Mountain Trench to Prince George where it changes direction and flows southwest toward the Pacific Ocean. By the time it arrives here at Hope, it has travelled thirteen hundred kilometres and is approximately forty metres above sea level. The freshet and high water arrive in June when snowmelt from the Interior mountains floods down.

At Hope, the Fraser changes direction again, turning from south to west in a wide arc at the waterfront. The life story of the Fraser is still being researched. Just why and when it changed direction are topics of scientific investigation. One theory says its course follows the Hozameen Ridge until that curls eastward around Mount Ogilvie. The river water then seeks the path of least resistance when it bumps into the harder igneous intrusions of the Skagit Range. Another theory suggests that valleys are sketched in by zones of weakness that follow fault lines, and that where the Fraser turns at Hope marks the junction of two fault lines.

The flat lands and the sandy river course here are the beginnings of the alluvial fan where the Fraser River starts to dump its load of sediment. To the west, the flats widen into a fertile valley flowing over several ancient beaches. The soil of today's Fraser Valley is more than a kilometre deep. The modern delta of the Fraser River estuary where sea tides mingle with fresh water begins around New Westminster. Every year the river carries three hundred cubic metres of sand, silt, and clay and deposits it into the sea 150 kilometres west of Landstrom Ridge. Thus, new land formation continues to happen today. Although humans alter the deposition of sediments in many ways, still, every year, the front of the delta is extended between three and nine metres, advancing three times as fast below sea level as on the surface. [Eisbacher] The mountains that once rose from the sea now return to the sea, transported in solution in the Fraser's golden sand-coloured water.

The Cascade Mountains on the south and east shore of the river are layers of eroded sediments to which a variety of volcanic and plutonic activity has added new landmass from below. They extended the continent west between one hundred million and fifty million years ago in the same way the Fraser extends the continent today. The oceanic plate continues to move towards land, subducting under, uplifting the continental plate, scrunching up the new sediments and new intrusions to create a new range of mountains sidling up to the old edge. These younger Coast Mountains sweep north from Vancouver and Hope to Yukon.

As it moves ever inward, the oceanic plate pushes some of its own landmass into a trench deep beneath the grinding plates. The abyss beyond the two plates connects to the Earth's hot core. In effect, the rim of plutonic and volcanic activity that created the Cascade Mountains was pushed underground, folded beneath the waves of new land. However, the openings between surfaces did not close completely. Nor did the inner fire die. Magma continues to roil and intrude upwards. Steam, heated waters, and lava still escape to the surface along this arc that is part of the Pacific Ring of Fire.

Sometimes activity beneath the crust is so powerful that eruptions occur. On May 18, 1980, Mount St. Helens, in the Cascade Mountains in southern

Washington State, exploded. Water vapour and hot gases under pressure burst through the side of the mountain and sent a "wind of stone" down the valley, flattening everything in its path. Then lava rolled down the truncated cone and into the glacial valley below. Fifty-seven people and countless wild animals died as a rain of ash settled over the continent. On other more ordinary days, the activity from the Earth's core results only in plumes of water vapour and gases escaping as they often do from the fumaroles on Mount Baker. Every day, hot water and minerals bubble to the surface at Harrison Hot Springs (thirty kilometres west of Hope) and at other hot springs along this volcanic arc, reminders of the mysteries at the Earth's core.

So, the Cascade volcanic arc remains active. After the North Cascades were created, or, as some geologists say, after the micro-continent attached itself to the continent [Alt], the end of the world did not stand still for long. New land formation continued as before. Erosion. Deposition. Intrusion. Extrusion. Subduction. Uplift. The waves of creation rolled in. Pieces of two-hundred-million-year-old ocean floor complete with marine fossils lie exposed adjacent to new rock of the Coast Mountains that is less than fifty million years old. The Coast Mountains are geologically younger than the Cascades, although the granite that melted and intruded to compose them may be much older than the actual mountains themselves. "The geology of the Cascade and southern Coast Ranges seems hopelessly complex . . . their history is like a book where most of the words are missing." [Cannings, GBC]

The Coast Mountains include Mount Waddington (4019 m), the tallest mountain completely in British Columbia, the Whistler/Blackcomb ski resort, Garibaldi Mountain, and the Golden Ears. The closest mountain in the Coast Range visible from Hope is Dog Mountain at the western end of the Fraser River Bridge. From Old Settler Mountain (2145 m) north of Ruby Creek, the nearest high Coast peak, you can see for miles. Eastward lie waves of land formed over the last 150 million years. Westward, the young Coast Mountains are less than fifty million years old. To the far west, less visible but still going on, new land is forming—by deposition, rifting, uplift—along the fiords and beaches of the West Coast.

At the first lookout on Landstrom Ridge, with the Fraser River below, the Cascades are south and east, the Coast Mountains north and west. However, no one in British Columbia gives directions in terms of cardinal compass points. Rivers wind, meander, double around, and change direction often. Roads use hairpin turns and switchbacks to reduce the incline. Only Right Turn or Left Turn is relevant. Or Up or Down, as the water flows. People travel "up country" or "up island" (north), "inland" or "over" to the Okanagan (east), or they go "down" to the Lower Mainland, referred to affectionately as "the wet coast" or "the Left Coast." Thus, although the signs on the highway up the Fraser Canyon may say #1 East, the compass should read

North. Eventually, the Trans-Canada reaches Halifax and the East Coast.

Another way direction is expressed locally is "green side" or "gold side." Green side refers to the west slope of the Cascades, where vegetation is rainforest fir, hemlock, and cedar over a lush understory. The gold side is the east slope of the Cascade Mountains, in the rainshadow, where precipitation is considerably less and vegetation more typically Ponderosa and lodgepole pine over shortgrass hills that turn gold and shimmer in the summer heat. In the town of Hope itself, you will also hear the expression "the sunny side." The old townsite is more exposed to the sun and wind. The season and proximity to the cliffs determine what hour of the day the sun will appear over or around the mountains. Yet all of Hope sits on the lush "green side," with 175 centimetres of rain annually, while our nearest neighbours to the east, Princeton or Merritt, both on the "gold side," receive thirty centimetres. In winter, Hope receives an additional 170 centimetres of snow.

ON-GOING CHANGE

"Rock of Ages, cleft for me.
Let me hide myself in thee."

—A. M. Toplady

On-Going Change

Fractures, Floods, and Rockfalls

On Landstrom Ridge, the trail, turning away from the cliff at the first lookout, climbs to the east. Ribbons mark important forks. The second lookout faces straight on to Silver Peak and Mount Isolillock, the Halkomelem word for "Mountain with Two Heads." Isolillock is also known as Holy Cross Mountain. From certain angles, when conditions are right, people see in the shape of the snowpack either a cross or an anchor. Local legend suggests that this symbol inspired the name for Fort Hope. The configuration signifies either hope of salvation or the security of a safe harbour (called a hope) that the bend in the river provides.

On Silver Peak, a slight snow cover highlights a straight line like a scar near the ridge between the two mountains. This line is the shadow of a narrow gauge railroad that once hauled ore out of a silver mine located high up the slope. Adits, the openings into abandoned mine shafts, ore cars, and the remains of the flume built to use gravity to get the ore down off the mountain, all tell the story. Here on Silver Peak, the first hardrock mine claim on the mainland in the colony of British Columbia was registered in 1868.

Although Silver Peak and Mount Isolillock seem to be related, linked by the saddle between them, the mountain with two heads is igneous while the other, to the left, is metamorphosed sedimentary rock. They are separated also by another interesting geologic feature. The Fraser-Straight Creek Fault Line, called the Straight Creek Fault Line in the United States, cuts right between the two peaks. The line comes down, skirting the western cliffs of Mount Hope, between Silver Creek and downtown Hope. It crosses, between Exits 168 and 170, outcrops of conglomerate rock with rounded river cobble and boulders visible, embedded in a metamorphosed red matrix that is as much as two hundred million years old (Mesozoic).

A straight-edged ruler on a roadmap, aligning Marblemount, Washington, with Boston Bar, traces the Straight Creek Fault Line. It cuts across the giant S-curve the Fraser River makes as it changes direction along the waterfront in Hope. It crosses the conglomerate again at the western end of the Fraser River Bridge, by Haig Station Road and the Canadian Pacific Railroad tracks, and continues due north, parallelling Ross Road, climbing with the Trans-Canada Highway for some distance. The line cuts through the Lake of the Woods, which was created during the last millennium when a mountain on the fault fell and water seeped over and collected in the tumble of boulders.

After the North Cascades micro-continent docked, around sixty-five million years ago, the new crust split or fractured into sections. The lines where the skin tore are called fault lines. Most run in a straight north-south line. It is believed that the faults reflect the stress put upon the continental plate by the oceanic plate pushing up and in from the southwest. The slice of the Cascade landform west of the Straight Creek Fault travelled 104 kilometres (sixty-eight miles) north of Hope, between one hundred and two hundred miles in total [Alt, RGW], in the twenty million years after it tore.

The Fraser-Straight Creek Fault Line, the biggest fault in southwestern British Columbia, probably accounts for the frequent rockslides in the Fraser Canyon. Yet, the Fraser-Straight Creek Fault Line is not active today. When the fault was moving, fifty million years ago, rocks on both sides were crushed. Those rocks still lack cohesion because of the twisting and pressure they experienced when the two sides were grinding along each other's edges. They shift and crumble more easily than solid rocks, but this is different from a movement in the fault itself. The Fraser-Straight Creek Fault Line is not presently active nor has there ever been any clustering of earthquakes along it. As further evidence of its inactivity, subsequent igneous intrusions have pushed through along the fault line and remain unmoved. [Alt, RGW] Unlike more well-known geologic faults, the Fraser-Straight Creek Fault Line is only a tear in the Earth's crust. In contrast, the San

Andreas Fault, the San Juan Fault, and the Queen Charlotte Fault west of the British Columbia coast, all associated with earthquake activity, mark places where two tectonic plates collide and pressures deep below are released by earth rumblings and quakes.

Fracturing may also cause topographic or surface changes in smaller ways. Triggered by weather, earthquakes, or human activity, segments of snow, rock, or mud may break off and slide or fall. Up Silverhope Creek, Silver Lake was created between 830 and 960 years ago when part of the mountain north of it fell into the valley. The rockfall raised the water level of the lake six or seven metres. Some of the fallen boulders can be seen at the exit channel where the lakewater flows into Silverhope Creek. "Historic landslides in British Columbia have been triggered by anomalous groundwater flow, high rainfall, freeze-thaw activity, and erosion of steep slopes by streams . . . Some large prehistoric landslide dams in this region may have formed during earthquakes. Radiocarbon dating of the dead trees in Silver Lake suggests that the Silver Lake rockfall postdates, although not by much, a major earthquake that triggered numerous landslides in the Seattle area, 190 kilometres south and west, 1000 to 1100 years ago." [Clague & Shilts]

Cheam Peak, forty kilometres west of Hope on the Trans-Canada freeway, stands as a sentry guarding the Upper Fraser Valley. Driving from Chilliwack towards Hope, Cheam's skirts are the curtains at the doorway, where the ascent into the Cascades begins. In 1872, an earthquake near the Washington border triggered a landslide from Cheam's north peak. Some of the tumbled rubble pile at her feet has since been transformed into Minter Gardens. *Cheam* is the Halkomelem word for "wild strawberry fields," a name applied to the lake at the piedmont and subsequently to the mountain itself. But the old Halkomelem name for Cheam, the mother mountain, is *Theeth-uhl-kay* [Wells] which translates as "the Source" or "the place from which the waters spring or slide."

With a skiff of snow-covering, the sedimentary layers on Mount Cheam are visible. Behind its peak, a long flat ridge rims the Fraser Valley south of Chilliwack. This is the Skagit Ridge, the old uplifted continental edge of the Skagit Range. Ancient streams and creeks are still visible today. They hang as glaciers or waterfalls like icicles dripping from the precipice. When the Cascades marked the edge of the continent, these streams off the Skagit Ridge ran into the ocean, either through the old channel of the Chilliwack River into what is now the Fraser River or via the Vedder River through Sumas Lake and the Nooksack River system to Bellingham Bay. A land reclamation project in the 1920s drained Sumas Lake; a system of dykes and canals shifted the Vedder River from the Nooksack to the Fraser River watershed.

Along the old continental edge in Hope, a natural change of water flow occurred at the beginning of the twentieth century. The old Hope townsite sits on the small alluvial fan, the delta where the Coquihalla River, pre and post glaciation, deposits its sediment as its waters meld with the Fraser waters on their way towards the Pacific. When the town was surveyed in 1859, the Coquihalla River curved around the base of Thacker and Ogilvie mountains and entered the Fraser about two kilometres farther north than the present confluence, past what is now called Lost Lagoon. In 1905, the Coquihalla changed its channel, pushing straight through from its confluence with Sucker Creek. [Dahl] Land between the old and new channel was lost, although some of it has since been reclaimed for the Hope Golf and Country Club. The golf course remains susceptible to flooding. Even annual events like high water cause on-going changes to the Earth's features.

An accident triggered another historic rockslide on the Fraser River in 1914. Blasting for a new railroad line on the east bank triggered the Hell's Gate disaster that crippled the salmon run for thirty years. Hell's Gate is a rock-walled gorge just south of Boston Bar in the Fraser Canyon. The Gate repeats the orogeny of the Fraser Canyon—metamorphosed sedimentary rock, on the left bank from the Cascades, on the right bank from the Coast Mountains, with the Fraser-Straight Creek Fault Line moving through. The sheer cliffs squeeze the river, already bolstered by the influx of the Thompson River at Lytton and the Nahatlatch north of Boston Bar, to a width of forty metres (120 feet). Low water is twenty-eight metres (eighty-five feet) deep; high water reaches a depth of up to fifty-eight metres (175 feet). The flow is seven metres (twenty feet) per second. Flung against the crags, the water swirls and eddies. The Gate was a popular but dangerous fishing spot for First Nations fishers using their dip nets from the rocks. The spawning salmon, two hundred kilometres from the sea on their homeward journey, are already tired before they have to tackle this maelstrom.

First Nations travellers avoided the waters of Hell's Gate. They climbed across vine and bark rope trellis ladders that they had strung from clifftop to waterline. Explorers Simon Fraser and George Simpson were grateful to have made it through the Canyon alive. Brigade packers, wagon road builders, Canadian Pacific railroad builders all tackled its challenge. When the new rail line, the Canadian Northern, blasted a single track and a series of tunnels on the east bank of the canyon, in 1911 and 1912, debris fell into the river and was removed. 1913 was the "Big Year" of the salmon's four-year cycle. British Columbia historian Bruce Hutchison in his book *The Fraser* tells it this way: "The railway debris had increased the speed of the river at the Gate, turned it into new courses deep below the surface, and created a cauldron which few fish could survive."

Since Great Britain still negotiated international affairs for Canada at that time, and salmon from ocean waters were a shared resource, both the Canadian and the British governments worked to clear the river that year. Then, on February 23, 1914, "a single slide from a railway tunnel on the east side of the Gate filled almost half the river channel." Frantic efforts helped some fish over the rapids, but the damage was not really corrected for thirty years when "ladders" called fishways were installed.

"Man had scoured the mountains of British Columbia for minerals, he had started to clean off the forests, but this depletion took time. In the Fraser, with a few sticks of dynamite, he had destroyed one of the precious food resources of mankind in a matter of minutes." [Hutchison] The number of First Nations upriver from the disaster who starved because the salmon did not return has never been adequately documented. The underlying sensitive issues—human dependence upon natural systems, and the tragic disruptions caused by man's unknowing interference—are still relevant. Today, Hell's Gate Airtram offers spectacular rides across the gorge, with views of the fishways and information about the history of this geologic feature and about the miracle of salmon cycles.

Snow falls, water freezes and thaws, rivers rise and flood, rocks and mud slide; change caused by natural forces continues to happen. Hope was the site of one of British Columbia's worst landslides, the Hope Slide. On January 9, 1965, a portion of Johnson Ridge, the uplifted old edge of the Hozameen Range, fell across the Hope-Princeton Highway sixteen kilometres east of town, close to the old Tashme Internment Camp. Four travellers who had stopped when a snow avalanche blocked the road were buried in their vehicles beneath the rock; two bodies were never recovered.

The slide fell into Outram Lake at the piedmont, which had been created by an earlier rockfall. The lake, when it received the mountain, splashed water and debris up the opposite side of the valley, wiping out all vegetation for several hundred metres. The highway was re-built through the rubble. The rocks remain, a testimony to the "ever-whirling wheel of change." The line where the water and mud reached up the opposite slope is still visible south of the highway in the new green of younger forest, below the older, established, and darker evergreens.

At the time of the Hope Slide, it was believed that a small earthquake nearby triggered the rockfall. "The seismograph record, originally thought to be an earthquake signal, is now known to be the sudden impact of the landslide debris on the valley floor." [Clague] January is a risky time of the year when temperature changes destabilize the snowpack. Freezing water becomes ice rock, which, because it expands, puts stress upon the other rocks into which it intrudes. Frost wedging causes rock to split; gravity helps it fall.

Mount Hope itself is deformed and faulting and prime for slides. In 1922, a rockfall from the north face blocked the old mill lead, a six-foot trench that had diverted water from the Coquihalla River to Hope's first sawmill, built in 1858 on the Fraser below what is now Exit 170. The mill itself, abandoned about the time Fort Hope closed in 1892, had been destroyed by the flood of 1894. At the same time as the mill lead was dammed by the rockfall, two adjacent cabins in the old red light district, near where Fourth Avenue meets the Old Hope-Princeton Way, were also destroyed. [Forging]

In November, 1995, after a period of heavy rainfall, a mudslide careened down Mount Hope, wiping out a business and closing down the freeway near Exit 170. Natural forces are constantly at play, shifting the surfaces or rumbling in the depths, extending land edges out, pushing some land masses up, and bringing other features down. Mountains rise from the sea and return to the sea. The only constant is change.

In 1999, fearing the damage that could be done if a rockfall landed on the railroad track, Canadian National Railway proceeded with prophylactic blasting of a peak in the Fraser Canyon near Yale. Putting safety before other concerns, the company had rushed to remove a hazard without seeking the appropriate consultation, especially from the Yale First Nation who live in the canyon. Elder Lawrence Hope spoke of his shock at the desecration: "It was like taking a cross off a church and chucking it on the ground. This is what we base our whole culture on." The jagged rock structure, tied to other sacred sites in the river nearby, was seen as a protector of the Yale people who were saddened at its destruction.

Such are the challenges when groups who understand things differently share the same land. Some people have an ear for the soul of stone; others fear the fall. Some revere rocks as places where spirit dwells; others read them differently, attuned to different stories. Some move mountains; others are moved by them. Some travel only on wheels or rails, their connection with the earth broken. Others enter the mountains on foot, sole to ground, in single file, approaching as pilgrims do, entering sacred space.

ON-GOING CHANGE

"Glaciers write with rock
on rock."

—Don McKay, "The Windchill Factor"
cited in *Fresh Tracks:
Writing the Western Landscape.*

On-Going Change

Glaciation

On Landstrom Ridge, the trail turns away from the peaks above Silver Creek and carries on. The third lookout faces the old Hope townsite where the fort once stood, with the waterfront and Greenwood Island in the foreground. Mount Hope looms right; the grey-white slash of the Hope-Princeton Highway snakes between green slopes. The point of Mount Macleod is snow-covered in the distance and Mount Ogilvie is the far left backdrop. If the conditions are right, Ogilvie's underlying layers of sediment are visible, especially on the columnar weathered cliff known as the Goat Bluff or the Tower. These layers of rock are the old edge of the continent. Those finger-like ridges of forested mountains radiating back behind Mount Ogilvie are uplifted cliff edges with eroded stream run-off channels above alluvial fans of sediment deposited at the rim of the continental plate.

The old townsite sits on its own delta, a triangle-shaped plain deposited between the feet of Mount Hope and Mount Ogilvie, where the Coquihalla River enters the Fraser River. The land is flat, sand, gravel, cobble and boulder sediment, previously cut by smaller creeks and streams, and subject to flooding. The mill lead from the Coquihalla River to the first sawmill at the bend in the Fraser would have followed an old rocky stream channel east of the fort. Greenwood Island, separated from shore by a narrow embrace of water, was a spit or sandbar at the lip of the delta that stabilized as soil and plant life accumulated.

In the green cliffs behind the town, a sand and gravel bluff rises above the houses. The many sand and gravel deposits in the landscape around Hope are visible evidence of glaciation. Next to the variety of rock formations, the thrill of living on a fault line, between the Cascades and the Coast Mountains, between the Hozameen and Skagit Ranges, along the old continent's edge, the most interesting local geologic features are those that offer clues about the movements of glaciers. Ice Ages are eras of slow spectacular change. However, once the ice has retreated into history, glaciation is in effect just another form of erosion.

For the last two million years, North America has experienced recurring Ice Ages when the land has been blanketed by a three-kilometre thickness of ice rock for periods of sixty to ninety thousand years at a time. At the height of Ice Ages, this continent was approximately thirty percent ice-covered. Today, ice still covers ten percent of the landmass. [Plummer *et al.*] The last massive glacier covered this section of the globe as recently, in geological time, as eleven thousand years ago. Some geologists theorize that the modern era is merely a transitional period between Ice Ages. There are seven hundred glaciers still on Cascade peaks today. Glaciers creep forward during winter and melt during summer. For most modern glaciers, the rate of receding exceeds the rate of advancing. The land is still rebounding as it recovers from the depressing weight of ice—rising four centimetres per year, the same rate as our fingernails grow. [Yorath]

Glaciation is very recent geologic action, and exposures touched by glacial ice are those on the surface where changes are more easily seen. During an Ice Age, immeasurable tonnes of frozen ice rock spread across the Earth's crust. Continental glaciers move down from the poles. However, in mountainous regions, glaciers move down from the heights, eroding valleys as they flow through them. When glaciers form in this region, snow falls and collects above the snowline; an ice cap forms; compressed ice squeezes out at the front edge and moves forward at a rate of metres per year, creeping down the trough between mountain ranges or the valleys between mountain ridges. In the face of an advancing glacier, human and other animal life retreats. The ice works as a giant eraser, rubbing away all evidence of pre-ice surface habitation. The weight of the ice depresses the land, which recovers, rebounds, after the glacier has melted.

The oppressive weight of ice rock moves, rounding the heads of hills and mountains it travels over in the interior plateau, surrounding high peaks, making them look like islands in a white sea, leaving their tips as unscarred nunataks. Creeping ice grinds down and carries away the crust, exposing granite plutons and batholiths. Ice scratches the walls of other rockfaces, scarring and truncating cliffs and outcrops. The glacier's load of gravel and boulders gouges the interface of earth and ice, leaving signature polished rock surfaces with often-parallel striations that record the direction of movement. Ice deepens valleys, changing their profile from a V to a U-shape, moving earth away from the sides, leaving some waterfalls hanging high above where once the tributary stream had met the river on the valley floor. Glaciers carve steps in underlying bedrock and benches along valley sides, and can leave mysterious caves, kettles, mounds, and deposits.

The front of the moving glacier tends to push a drift of loose rocks and till, unsorted and unlayered rock debris. The drift is often horseshoe-shaped as it conforms to the front and sides of the tongue of ice filling the mountain trough. When the glacier stops, the drift of rocks, called a terminal moraine, remains as a sign of the extent of the glacier's southward or downward movement. As the glacier begins melting and retreating, it deposits a recessional moraine at each place it pauses. Lateral moraines remain where the sides of glaciers used to be and medial moraines build up where two glaciers flow into each other. Along with the drift and till, smaller particles are washed out with the glacial melt and accumulate downstream from the terminus of the glacier. These outwash deposits of sand show evidence of stream layering.

Glaciation affects sea levels. During a major ice age, so much water is frozen that the sea level drops. Conversely, in smaller regions, with alpine glaciers as opposed to continental ice sheets, the weight of the glacier pushes down the land and seawater moves farther inland. As the glacier recedes, the depression lessens, land rebounds and sea retreats. Meltwater carries sediment farther out into the ocean, building up new land. At the end of the last Ice Age, about eleven thousand years ago, the sea reached in from Bellingham Bay towards Agassiz and in from Boundary Bay as far east as Pitt Lake. [Cannings, GBC]

Around Hope, ice wrought changes in the rivers, tributaries, valleys, and canyons, in the deposits of sand, gravel, and clay; in the soil that sustains vegetation; in elevation and sea level. Where the valley flowing down from the gap between Silver Peak and Isolillock wraps around Mount Hope, over the inactive fault line, just south of Old Yale Road, there is an impressive sandpit with grains so large that their jagged glacial (not waterborne) origins are visible to the naked eye. Above the pit, the steep vertical cliffs of Mount Hope are scarred and gouged; huge chunks have been torn away, leaving once-rounded rockfaces truncated, rubbed smooth and flat. A glacier slunk here very recently. The cross-bedded layers of sand are glacial outwash.

North from downtown Hope, across the Coquihalla

River Bridge, down Kawkawa Lake Road towards the end of Kettle Valley Road, or down Othello Road, heading for the tunnels, roads cross a wide band of sand and gravel that is pit-mined for use in construction. This huge deposit of gravel, the sidehill visible from the third lookout, is a moraine from the last glacier.

A glacier also created the kettle that is now Kawkawa Lake. A kettle is a depression formed underneath a glacier. Perhaps a calf from the glacier fell off and was run over, buried beneath the advancing ice sheet, and glacial till was deposited around this ice chunk, forming a cast. The ice plug preserves the depression or hollow. Alternatively, "when a glacier melts and draws away from an area, a block of ice may break off and be covered by earth and rock. As the block melts, the ground above it subsides, forming a kettle." [TCE] The depression that is now Kawkawa Lake is a kettle filled with spring water. Two dry kettles flank the water-filled one along this old glacier path.

The glacier in this valley was so huge that it dammed the original course of the Coquihalla River which used to wind around the base of Mount Ogilvie, either straight through Kawkawa Lake to the Fraser or around, through what is now Thacker Marsh and Sucker Creek, circling the base of Thacker Mountain. With its natural route blocked by ice and gravel, the Coquihalla was forced to seek a new, more difficult route. The river ate through the spectacular granite-walled Coquihalla Canyon, where Rambo hid from his pursuers in *First Blood*.

In 1999, Aberfoyle Springs tapped the vestigial pre-glacial Coquihalla River to bottle water from the aquifer on the ancient riverbed below metres of glacial deposits. The company, which has since sold to Perrier, built a bottling factory where a natural spring trickles up from the floor of the valley between Othello Road and Kawkawa Lake. On a contour map [Hope 92 H/6], the wet and dry kettles appear as irregular shapes amid the wide strand of low land between the two rivers that is the old glacier valley.

There is a third, active sand quarry in Hope, at the end of Ross Road close to Haig Station, on Schkam/Chawathil Reserve land. The sand in this pit, which is high on a cliff on the northwest, right bank of the Fraser, contains a mixture of river-borne and glacial-washed silica. From the locations of these three sand deposits, geologists can tell that three glaciers at least must have crept towards Hope, probably down the ancient Coquihalla rivercourse, the Silverhope Creek floodplain, and the Fraser waterway. When, in what order, and whether they ever met, is not yet known.

Inland, in the Hozameen Range of the Cascade Mountains along Coquihalla Pass, in a line behind the gravel cliff overlooking the town, there is more evidence of glacial activity. The several peaks of the Zopkios Ridge, near the tollbooths on the Coquihalla Highway, are an igneous formation called the Plutonic Belt. This granite batholith began as molten rock intruding up beneath the crust and cooling underground. Then the old crust layer was eroded away with the help of as many as four different glaciers advancing and retreating over successive Ice Ages. The abrasive glaciers polished the granite rock to a sheen and gouged out striations on its surface. Subsequent water and ice erosion caused exfoliation. The polished surface cracks and flakes off like dry skin.

Needle Peak near the Coquihalla Summit beckons like a finger, inviting climbers to explore its smooth slopes poking out of the crushed scree and till below. Sometimes sharp peaks similar to the Needle suggest that glaciers moved around the formation instead of over top, leaving the peak as a nunatak. Some peaks are created simply when unsupported rock below them detaches and drops. Alternatively, a finger may be formed when frost wedges out chunks of rock, which are then plucked away from the side adjacent to the flow. A cirque, a circular basin-like depression found in rock above the snowline, is caused by the combined forces of freezing, expansion of water as it turns to ice, wedging, thawing, and gravity which causes the broken rock to fall away. If a depression fills with water, it forms a tarn or mountain lake.

The glaciers moved millions of tonnes of sand and gravel from all along their route through the central interior of the province and deposited it as till or sediment. Large boulders were picked up and dropped elsewhere as erratics. Smaller and looser glacial deposits, drift or till, are characteristically scattered rather than layered, jagged-edged rather than smooth, and of varied composition because they were acquired from different sources. Water crossing such deposits picks them up, tumbles them smooth, sorts them by weight, and drops them elsewhere, creating boulder-bedded streams above sandbars and deltas like the one Hope occupies. Through combinations of river depth, bank composition, and the actions of current and wind, sandbars grow. Heavier rocks and minerals settle out on the bars that are also, historically, sources of gold and jade in this region.

Soil and sand deposited on the rocks and sandbars hold moisture and nurture plant life. The one-sided trees on Landstrom Ridge and on the Hope waterfront have been carved by the wind. The Fraser Valley acts as a funnel, bringing the Pacific airshed inland. Prevailing westerly winds rush from the coast to this bend in the river. Wind action on the trees is visible; its action on the water, confusing and slowing it where the air riffles the surface, helps initiate deposition of sediments. The hot winds of summer have been used for millennia by First Nations people drying their salmon. In winter, the winds reverse; the canyon channels a cold outflow south.

On Landstrom Ridge, the trail continues north to the fourth lookout that faces towards the cliffs marking the beginning of the Fraser Canyon. Twenty-five kilometres up river, straight north along the fault line, the town of Yale marks the head of navigation on the Fraser River. Even today, the waters of the Fraser are considered uncharted. This does not mean that no one has ever mapped them. It means that the sandbars are so elusive, shifting with every swish of the current, every rise or fall of water level, that it is impossible—misleading and dangerous—to attempt to locate them on a map. At Yale, the current becomes too swift, the encroaching rock-faces too threatening, for most watercraft other than adventure rafters.

The valley of the Fraser between Yale and Hope offers more examples of the effects of glacial action upon landscape. Glaciers carved a wide bench along the Fraser's east bank and eroded the sides of the valley into the typical U-shape, leaving many streams hanging. This U-shape is clearly visible from the Spirit Caves Trail above Yale. However, more than surface features, the glaciers may also have changed the course of the river itself. The Fraser Canyon walls may be so sheer because this canyon too is very young. John Clague, formerly of the Geological Survey of Canada, says: "The issue of whether the Fraser River flowed through the Fraser Canyon before the Ice Ages is an interesting one. At one time (perhaps ten to twenty million years ago), the drainage in central BC was northerly and easterly, towards Alberta. The proto-Fraser River probably flowed north past what is now Quesnel. Some time later, but we don't know when, the drainage changed and the Fraser became established in its present course. The cause of this change in drainage is unknown but may be connected with glaciation or mountain building."

The story of this place called Hope is a story of transformation. Many changes have happened here, either slowly, over millions or thousands of years, or suddenly, in a matter of seconds. Whether fast or slow, they continue to happen. Earth's is an on-going story. Rain and snow fell and mountains moved before

ind arrived. Rain and snow continue to fall,
mountains are moving still. The influx of earth-
humans into the region has been responsible
the most recent topographic changes.

dstrom Ridge takes hikers backwards in historic
ogic time as they climb. Walking the ridge,
gazing from its lookouts, helps tune the ear to listen,
train the eye to read the rocks. From the fourth lookout,
the trail circles back to where it began. Some pilgrims
say thank you, or offer a benediction, when they come
down off the rock, before they carry on. For there is
still more to see. Every stone has a story to tell.

On-Going Change

"At the beginning of the world
. . . Coyote walked up the Canyon
from the mudflats at Hope
. . . one by one singing
the monsters who lived there
into stone."

—Harold Rhenisch,
from *Tom Thomson's Shack*

On-Going Change

First Nations (Telte Yet Campsite)

Crossing the Fraser River, entering Hope from the west, travellers are invited, by a stand of tall cedar trees along the waterfront, into the Telte Yet Campsite. Telte Yet means "the up river people"; this campsite occupies land reserved for First Nations. There are other pockets of reserve land—on the back of Thacker Mountain, on Union Bar, up the east side of the Fraser, on the cliffs overlooking the river on the west bank, up river towards Yale, and down river on both sides. Traditional territory, land claimed by First Nations, extends far back from the river into the mountains. Cedar and other plants rooted to the rocks, and animals living on them or in the water, have sustained the Sto:Lo, the People of the River, for millennia. From the rocks, they still dip their nets into pools of salmon, or draw nets across the current, and hang their catch to dry in hot summer winds on racks along the shore.

The First Nations who shared this territory before contact with Europeans trod softly, leaving only traces of their presence—worn trails, the pits of abandoned houses, quarries, culturally altered rocks used for tools or for ritual or decorative purposes. In *Forging A New Hope,* pioneer Mrs. Edmond Lorenzetto, whose great-grandfather was Chief Wallace of Agassiz, documents how old totem poles with eagle and bear crests were chopped down and incorporated into a house and then a barn which was later burned on purpose. Many facets of First Nations culture are ephemeral, or intangible. However, landscape offers a more permanent record. Some names are descriptive, recording geologic or other natural features. Mount Ogilvie was "many breasted" while Hope was "the place of skinned rocks" where the current and water fluctuations kept shorelines free of moss. Some names commemorate mythological beings or ancestral spirits, narratives attached to place, transcribed in stone.

Transformer Rocks, such as the rock celebrated at Hatzic along the north shore of the Fraser River east of Mission, remember legends about mythic ancestors such as Hal who preceded today's people (who still speak Halkomelem, the language of Hal's people). Transformers were sorcerers or shamans who often participated in competitive duels with other powerful combatants. The losers, transformed by their adversaries into stone and tossed on the bank or into the river as an eternal reminder to the people, were admonished: "You stay there forever." [Wells, CTN] Spirit dwells there still. The huge rock in the middle of the Fraser River above Yale is one such Transformer Rock. It's name, *xeyl-xel-em-as* to downriver sources, refers to the many-eyes of the river monster transformed there. Landscape features thus spark story or legend, keeping the names of the ancestors or of the vanquished enemies alive in memory. Moreover, landscape is part of a living sacred universe. Humans are connected to that landscape through nominative tacks or by narrative lines. People are expected to behave in a suitably reverent manner, with respect towards the physical world and towards the spirit that resides therein.

Transformer legends are part of the culture of both First Nations groups who live in this region. One explanation for the meaning of Coquihalla says it is a Nlaka'pamux name for a powerful Nicola ancestor, Coqua-Halla, who, jealous or angered by humans who refused to obey him, transformed the men who were hunting and the women who were picking berries into dolomite pillars and tossed them to opposite sides of his valley. Yet another derivation says that the name is a Halkomelem word which translates as "stingy container" or "stingy with the fish" and refers to legends of the little people who steal fish from nets in the river's swirling waters. [Hill, EKVR]

First Nations people routinely linked stories to observed geologic features in the landscape. Archaeologists in *They Write Their Dreams on the Rock Forever* note that many of the petroglyph and pictograph sites in the Fraser and Stein River valleys are located where veins of white rock such as quartz or deposits such as calcium carbonate are visible. They cite Teit: "White was a 'spirit' colour and stood for ghosts, spirit world, dead people, skeletons, bones, sickness, coming from the dead." The streaks on rocks are interpreted as marks of power and are thus sought out by dreamers and questers as places to receive and record their own visions and songs, and by hunters or travellers as places to make an offering and seek protection on their journey.

At home as they were in this living place, First Nations hunters and gatherers of this region also knew where to find flint, chert, and other rocks whose concoidal fracturing makes chipping to a sharp edge easier. The name Hozameen, a mountain range, a ridge, and an individual peak just across the American border, is a Nlaka'pamux word meaning "sharp like a knife" and may refer either to the sharp uplifted ridge or to the chert mines where many groups procured raw rock material for tool-making. They also crafted jade, soapstone, granite, or other rocks into beautiful tools, ceremonial, and decorative objects. They knew where visible veins or outcrops of different coloured minerals were located. Local First Nations traded native copper nuggets with coastal groups who prized it. They gathered gold nuggets and took them to the nearest post to trade.

The first discovery of gold on the mainland is contested; the Columbia River, Fort Kamloops, Alexandria House, and Fort Hope all claim some credit. [Shewchuk] It is known that Governor Douglas in Victoria liked to pass bottles of gold dust around the factor's table and predict that the world as the Hudson's Bay Company had known it would soon change. [Adams] Whether or not they were the first, in 1857, a First Nations family, camped where Nicoamen Creek enters the Thompson River, found a huge gold nugget. They took it into the Hudson's Bay trading post where it was forwarded to Fort Victoria and then to the Company's banking facility in San Francisco. The find triggered the Fraser River Gold Rush and thus, indirectly, with the flood of non-British subjects into pre-colonial territory, the establishment of the colony and then of the province of British Columbia.

First Nations had well-established trails through the mountains and canyons. They knew how to follow the lead of the waterways, and where to go overland to make the connection between one watershed and the next. Because the sources of stone tools can be traced— to obsidian mines in Oregon, for instance, or to the chert caves in the Skagit Valley—the distribution of artifacts provides evidence that local First Nations traded with people both from the north and far to the south. The Sto:Lo also traded goods they had crafted such as woven rush or cedar mats, capes, hats, baskets, and wool blankets hand-loomed from spun mountain goat hair or the hair of domestic dogs kept for that purpose. They manufactured dugout log canoes and carved totem poles, wooden boxes, grave goods, and ceremonial masks. They also decorated their houses and the tools they used for fishing, spinning, or weaving. Many Sto:Lo relics, received as gifts or otherwise acquired, are found in museums around the world.

The Sto:Lo, Halkomelem-speakers, lived in winter settlements, in family or communal houses, before European contact, and moved seasonally to camps for fishing. They shared overlapping territory with neighbouring groups and resolved disputes in front of witnesses at large public longhouse gatherings. At these potlatches or winter dances, the oral history was recited and ritual gift-giving accompanied ceremonies of remembrance, naming, or inheritance. Initiates being trained in tenets of the culture spent darks nights alone, in the longhouses, or at pools, waterfalls, rock caves, or other power places on the mountains as they prepared themselves to commence a spiritual life, to share their song and dance with the guests at the feast in the big house. First Nations tended to form strategic alliances through trade and inter-marriage with potentially threatening neighbours such as the Nlaka'pamux (Thompson) to the north whose territory reached as far south as Spuzzum, or the Interior Salish of the Okanagan, and with their Coast Salish Halkomelem-speaking relatives to the west and south.

At the potlatches, the chief and family sponsoring the event would give away possessions they had gathered or manufactured to honoured guests invited to witness the ceremony. To accumulate a feast's supply of blankets, carved objects, utensils, and food, a family had to have a wealth of relatives working in consort to gather, hunt, fish, spin, weave, carve, manufacture, trade, and cook. The giving-away, only partly an economic system, affirmed personal power and political connections. It was also important as a social activity,

Fraser River from the First Lookout on Landstrom Ridge, 150 kilometres upriver from Vancouver. Coast Mountains to the right; Cascade Mountains to the left.

Photo: J. M. Bridgeman

Photo: J. M. Bridgeman

From the Second Lookout on Landstrom Ridge. Silver Peak and Mount Isolillock in the Skagit Range of the Cascade Mountains overlooking Silver Creek.

Mount Hope, here behind the wind-carved trees on Landstrom Ridge, is a granite pluton in the Skagit Range of the Cascade Mountains.

Photo: J. M. Bridgeman

Photo: J. M. Bridgeman

From the Third Lookout on Landstrom Ridge. Mount Hope to the right. Mount Macleod (in clouds) and peaks including Mount Ogilvie to the left are part of the Hozameen Range of the Cascade Mountains. Fort Hope was built across from Greenwood Island, along the waterfront where the Fraser River changes direction.

Mountains formed in water—sediments
deposited at the continent's edge
metamorphosed, uplifted, and eroded.
Right: Thacker Mountain Fold.
Below: Jones Lake.

Photo: J. M. Bridgeman

Photo: Rick Easterbrook, Perceptions

83

Water cascades over granite tiers of an eroded pluton in the Skagit Range at Flood Falls, near Exit 165 of the Trans-Canada Highway.

Photo: J. M. Bridgeman

Photo: John Riley, Wilderness Therapy

Waves of mountains, from sediments deposited, metamorphosed, uplifted, intruded by igneous plutons, or pierced by extruded volcanic cones. The peaks of the Skagit Range of the Cascades, including snow-capped Mount Baker, seen from Mount Outram in the Hozameen Range.

Photo: Jenny Wolpert

The Coquihalla Highway,
which opened in 1986,
crosses the Plutonic Belt of
the Hozameen Range, skirting
this glacier-polished batholith.

Freezing, thawing, ice
wedging, and gravity help
erode granite exposures
and feed tarns such as this
one southwest of Needle
Peak in the Coquihalla
Plutonic Belt.

Photo: Jenny Wolpert

When glacial ice blocked the water's usual route, the Coquihalla River carved a new channel through intruded granite in the Coquihalla Canyon.

Photo: Rick Easterbrook, Perceptions

Photo: J. M. Bridgeman

Lava extruded above the earth's crust and engulfed water-rounded river cobble to form conglomerate such as this seen here along Ross Road.

The Hope Slide. Johnson Ridge fell
into the valley January 9, 1965.

Coquihalla granite polished by a glacier,
with striations visible in the upper centre,
and exfoliation at the top.

Cross-bedded strata in gravel pits, on Kettle Valley Road and behind Old Yale Road, suggest stream activity in outwash from glacial moraines.

Old Settler in the Coast Mountains. The jagged-edged boulders of varied composition suggest that they were picked up by a moving glacier at different locations and transported before being dropped as drift. These tarns could have been formed as kettles under the ice.

Photo: Jenny Wolpert

Kawkawa Lake is a kettle created by a glacier.

Photo: John Riley, Wilderness Therapy

89

Indian fishing on the Fraser River near Yale. From the rocks, the Sto:Lo, People of the River, have fished for salmon for millennia.

Fort Hope. Around Hope, rocks make the rivers unnavigable and mountains make overland travel difficult. In 1848, the Hudson's Bay Company built Fort Hope north of the new International Boundary to be closer to the trailheads to transport goods to and from Interior posts. The same wind-carved firs line the waterfront today.

Rider on the Hope-Merritt Trail.
After 1848, the Hudson's Bay Company sought accessible land routes through the Cascades. Brigade trails were paths wide enough for trains of mules and horses carrying packs. By the 1870s, ranchers were driving cattle between the coast and the interior along similar trails.

Miners gold panning near Yale. In 1858, the Fraser River Gold Rush brought thousands of miners into the territory to pan or sluice the sand and gravel deposits for metal flushed from the rocks. HBC officials pushed for colonial status and the establishment of British institutions to ensure public safety.

Cariboo Road, Fraser River. In 1861, the discovery cf gold in the Cariboo resulted in a re-deployment of Royal Engineers and contractors to build a wagon road north, first from Port Douglas to Lillooet, the Douglas Road, and then from Yale to Barkerville, the Cariboo Wagon Road.

Excursion train above Yale during CPR construction, June 1885. In 1871, British Columbia, which had become a united colony in 1866, joined the Canadian Confederation as a province on the promise of a railroad linking west to east. Construction finally began through the Fraser Canyon when the contractor, Andrew Onderdonk, moved his headquarters to Yale in 1880.

1914—Construction of a second railroad along the left bank of the Fraser caused landslides at Hell's Gate which destroyed the salmon run for thirty years. From the air-tram, the fishways are visible (bottom left) as are the shear rock walls and the swirl of the current which caused such difficulty for Simon Fraser in 1808 and George Simpson in 1828.

1911-1916—Andrew McCulloch blasted the KVR through granite at the Othello Tunnels in the Coquihalla Canyon. The Othello Tunnels have now been transformed into a park and recreational area. A slide wiped out the work camp at the Ladner Creek Tunnel (right) and delayed the opening of the KVR in 1915. The crumbling sediments have blocked the tunnel again; the trail to the trestle goes over the top.

In 1915, the Kettle Valley Railroad from Midway to Hope, in co-operation with the provincial government, built the first bridge across the Fraser River at Hope. Trains crossed to the CPR main line on the lower level. Automobiles crossed on the upper deck.

In 1927, the Fraser Canyon section of the Trans-Canada Highway opened, with a toll at Alexandra Bridge

In the 1940s, the Silver Skagit Logging Company, based in Silver Creek, logged the Skagit Valley in anticipation of the construction of the High Ross Dam on the Skagit River in Washington State.

Low water on the Fraser River at the confluence with the Coquihalla River. (Notice the rockhounds.)

High water on the Fraser River at the confluence with the Coquihalla River. The freshet arrives in June.

Rockhounds assume the pilgrim posture in the cobble where the Coquihalla River enters the Fraser River here in Hope. Hozameen Range to the left; Skagit Range to the right.

bringing large gatherings and all generations together. As a spiritual ceremony, potlatches assured, in the presence of witnesses, that the culture would remain strong.

Perhaps misunderstanding the purposes of the give-aways, or perhaps understanding all too well and hoping to curtail such activities as a way to enforce assimilation of First Nations people, the Canadian government passed laws in 1884 making the feasts illegal. Laws against the potlatches struck at the very roots of West Coast First Nations culture. Sto:Lo chiefs wore their woven blankets, symbols of their wealth and status equal to the ermine-trimmed robes of European monarchs, when they went to London to petition the King to defend their rights against the federal government in 1912. Their appeal to the higher authority was unsuccessful at that time; the Potlatch Laws were not repealed until 1951. Mistrust of federal motives has not gone away, although the Canadian Charter of Rights and Freedoms should guarantee that no such interference with the rights of individuals or groups could happen again.

Because the glaciers erased pre-Ice Age surface traces, physical evidence of human habitation goes back only about ten thousand years in this region. The oral history of First Nations includes creation myths that explain, spiritually and psychologically, how human beings first came to this land. In some stories, humans arrive from the sky. In others, they emerge from the sea, or are formed from the mud of the earth, or carved from the trunk of a tree. Such origins recognize our vital connection to the natural world, which is both raw material for and conduit of humankind. "Everything on the Earth is of the Earth," the Elders say. "The Earth does not belong to man; man belongs to the Earth," Chief Seattle asserted a century ago.

Today, the old theory that humans peopled North America by walking across the Bering Strait landbridge is questioned. Eurocentric and possibly self-serving, this proposition makes First Nations just another group of immigrants and fits them into a world view based upon Middle Eastern Judeo-Christian creation myth. Who can say that people from the Americas did not populate Asia and Europe? A bridge goes both ways. Science is not necessarily objective. Psychological truths are significant; judicial rulings insist that oral tradition must also be given credence.

What can the people who were first here, who have known this land the longest, teach the rest of us about how to survive, to lead a good life, in this landscape? What is really important? What can we learn from each other about how to live in this universe?

ON-GOING CHANGE

"The whole earth is a great tablet
holding the multiple overlaid
new and ancient traces of the swirl of forces."

—Gary Snyder,
"The Place, the Region, and the Commons"
from *The Practice of the Wild.*

Sunlight over the Hozameen Ridge of the old continent's edge spills on to a Transformer Rock re-named to honour Lady Franklin, at the head of navigation on the Fraser River in Yale.

On-Going Change

Exploration, Forts, and Trails (Cairn)

Along the waterfront from the Telte Yet campground, a historic cairn in Centennial Park commemorates the beginnings of European settlement at Hope. Although some records in Chinese archives and some archaeological evidence indicates early Asian contact with the Americas, written history still begins with the arrival of European explorers and traders. European contact along this West Coast began with the Spanish who explored from their establishments in Mexico in the sixteenth century. It is possible that Sir Francis Drake also reached these shores when he was circumnavigating the globe in the 1570s, claiming it for Queen Elizabeth I and naming it New Albion.

Spanish interest in the NorthWest increased after Russian explorers established trading posts in the eighteenth century. Jose Maria Narvaez surveyed the mouth of the Fraser for the Spanish Navy in 1791. The

English were still looking for a NorthWest Passage through North America at that time. Captain Cook traded on Vancouver Island; his explorations in the 1770s led to Captain George Vancouver's detailed mapping of the coast from 1792 to 1794. Captain Vancouver, safe on a bobbing ship, his eye glued to the huge lens of a telescope, peering inland into the green wall of trees, missed the mouth of the Fraser in the fog. He did name Mount St. Helens (for a British diplomat), and Mount Baker (after Lieutenant Baker, the man on his crew who first spied the peak), and Puget Sound (after Lieutenant Peter Puget). However, Captain Vancouver, who established neither a trading post nor a settlement, would not have seen Mount Hope. The City of Vancouver, incorporated and re-named in 1886 to commemorate the British explorer, did not exist before 1867. It had grown from a tavern along the waterfront established by Captain "Gassy" Jack Deighton, a Yorkshireman who had arrived for the gold rush and had piloted steamboats on Harrison Lake and on the Fraser River between New Westminster and Fort Hope.

European contact with northern North America began on the East Coast and worked its way westward. The Vikings built a settlement which they later abandoned in Newfoundland a millennium ago. Portuguese, Spanish, and Italian sailors returned in the late fifteenth century, coming initially *en route* to India and coming back for the fish and then for the furs. France claimed land along the St. Laurence River in the sixteenth century and founded the settlement that would become Quebec City in 1608. By the eighteenth century, fur traders from the North West Company, headquartered in Montreal, and from the Hudson's Bay Company, chartered in 1670 and headquartered in London, England, were exploring rivers that flowed towards the oceans. Water remained the preferred mode of transportation. Forts were, for the most part, outposts in the wilderness whose sole purpose was economic—the trans-shipping of traded and trading goods.

In 1745, the LaVerendryes glimpsed the Rocky Mountains from the east. Alexander Mackenzie explored the headwaters of the Peace River, crossed the Rocky Mountains and, travelling overland, reached the Pacific Ocean "from Canada by land" in 1793. He travelled down the Fraser as far as the West Road River between Prince George and Quesnel. Taking his guides' advice that turning west was the shortest, safest, and fastest route to the sea, he arrived at salt water along the Dean Channel, west of Williams Lake. The First Nations people also told him that other white people were already building a town three days down the coast. Mackenzie thought that the river he travelled south on had been the Columbia and that someone else would have to follow that river south.

The river Mackenzie had abandoned was explored to its mouth by Simon Fraser in 1808. Fraser was born in 1776 in New Hampshire of Scottish immigrant parents. His father had been active for the Royalists and died in prison during the American Revolutionary War. As a Loyalist, Fraser moved with his mother to

Quebec in 1783 and apprenticed as a clerk with the North West Company in 1792. In 1804, scouting for a planned expansion into new trading territory, he crossed the Rocky Mountains. He called this region New Caledonia because it looked like the Scotland his homesick mother had described to him in his youth.

In May, 1808, Simon Fraser set out from Fort George to descend the river that he too thought was the Columbia. By June 26, their group of twenty-four had reached Hell's Gate. Fraser noted in his Journal the footpaths worn into the bedrock on the top of the bluffs, "impressed, indented upon the very rocks by frequent travelling." They followed their guides, climbing across the trellis ladders of poles, twigs, and withes attached to the canyon walls over-hanging the maelstrom. "We had to pass where no human being should venture," Fraser wrote. People camped near Yale entertained him and provided food. In the granite cliff near their fish drying racks: "They shewed us indented marks which the white people made upon the rocks, but which by the bye, seemed to us to be natural marks."

Fraser floated past Hope during high water on June 29. From the waterfront here, the S-curve in the river is easy to see. For Fraser, the radical change in direction was disturbing. Something was not right. The next day, one of his men took a reading and confirmed that they were drifting west rather than south. Knowing the global positioning of the Columbia River mouth, Fraser realized his group was too far north. On July 3, near Musqueam at the mouth of the river, they turned around. There, at saltwater, the readings did not jibe, and Fraser had to admit that he was not on the Columbia and that all his hard and dangerous work had been for naught. Although the descent had taken thirty-six days, the party returned upstream, paddling against the fast current, in thirty-five days, aided perhaps by Fraser's handling of his crew's near mutiny, and the fact that they feared for their lives from now-hostile encampments. Of his journey in general, Fraser's attitude was: "Our situation is critical and highly unpleasant." However, he set an example by endeavouring to make the best of it. "[W]hat cannot be cured must be endured."

Fraser reported to his superiors that the river was not navigable and that a more accessible route would have to be found to supply the new forts the company planned to construct west of the Rocky Mountains. His friend, the cartographer David Thompson, named the mighty river "Frazer's" River in 1813, but for Simon Fraser it was forever the River of Disappointment.

The Columbia, the River of the West that Mackenzie and Fraser sought, provides the only water access from the ocean to the Interior. Draining one of the largest watersheds on the continent, the Columbia flows for 1950 kilometres from its headwaters in eastern British Columbia. In Washington State, the river makes a wide arc around the shield volcanoes of the Columbia Plateau. As the only river to go through the Cascade Mountains, the Columbia cuts a deep gorge along a line that now divides Oregon from Washington State.

Americans had already explored the southern reaches of the Columbia before Simon Fraser crossed the Rockies. In 1792, Robert Gray, a sea captain from Boston, entered the mouth of the Columbia from the Pacific Ocean and named the river in honour of his ship *Columbia*, (from *columb*, meaning "dove.") The area around the river, between Russian and Spanish territory, became known as the Columbia Region.

British and American interests competed for the Columbia Region. From 1804 to 1806, Lewis and Clark, dispatched by President Thomas Jefferson, trekked overland to the Pacific Ocean, exploring the Louisiana Purchase. They over-wintered in the rains at the mouth of the Columbia in absolute misery, but they returned with maps and word of great resources, preparing the way for settlement and territorial status within the next fifty years. Fur trading posts sprang up along the Columbia and its tributaries. When David Thompson, exploring for the North West Company, reached its mouth from the north in 1811, he found Americans already there, at Fort Astoria. Coming up the Columbia and the Okanogan (American spelling) rivers, traders moved into the Okanagan Valley and thence overland to Kamloops where Americans built a fort in 1812.

British and American traders, vying for the same territory, and often building across the river from each other, tried to convince the resident First Nations to bring furs to their forts. After the two "British" companies amalgamated in 1821, the Hudson's Bay Company built headquarters at Fort Vancouver, in

1825, on the opposite bank from Fort Astoria and several kilometres upriver. However, the writing was on the canyon walls. Politicians and traders both knew that the dispute over who owned the Columbia Region would have to be resolved soon.

George Simpson, an independent and driven Scot, was appointed Governor of the amalgamated Hudson's Bay Company after 1821 and ran it like a czar for forty years. Simpson was sceptical of Simon Fraser's conclusions about the river that he had explored. The "Little Emperor" could not believe any waterway could be that unnavigable; he suspected Fraser of shirking. Simpson was not merely being contrary. He had travelled most of the brigade routes used by the Company. As part of his supervisory duties, he visited every post and attended the annual councils of each district. In all other parts of Canada, the brigade routes followed waterways. The annual shipments of trading goods to the posts and traded goods to headquarters travelled as large packs loaded on convoys of canoes or York boats. Packs and vessels were carried around whitewater over portages (from the French *porter*, to carry). Only in British Columbia, where rivers were not always navigable, were the packs transferred to horseback. The brigades became pack trains and the brigade routes became pack trails. The main brigade route from northern forts such as Fort St. James left the Fraser River at Alexandria for an overland trail to Fort Kamloops that continued south through the highlands of the Cascades, west of the Okanagan Valley, to Fort Okanogan on the Columbia River.

In 1828, Simpson determined to check Frazer's River out himself. At Hell's Gate, Simpson, who was attempting the passage at a relatively safer low water level, with the best paddlers in the country, convinced himself that "this requires more confidence than skill," and led his men and canoes into the narrow canyon. "The banks now erected themselves, into perpendicular Mountains of Rock from the Waters edge, the tops enveloped in clouds, and the lower parts dismal and rugged in the extreme," he wrote in his Dispatch to the Governor and Committee in London. It was like going in blind, he explained. Once the current grabbed their canoe, they could no longer control it. There were no places to stop and reconnoiter. "Our craft would shoot like an arrow into deep whirlpools, which seemed to sport in twirling us about." Simpson emerged from the Hell's Gate abyss with a total change of attitude. He had learned through unhappy experience that Fraser had indeed been correct.

"Frazer's River, can no longer be thought of as a practicable communication with the interior. . . . I should consider the passage down, to be certain Death, in nine attempts out of Ten." Simpson at least was able to learn from his experience. "I shall therefore no longer talk of it as a navigable stream, altho' for years past I had flattered myself with the idea, that the loss of the Columbia would in reality be of very little consequence to the Honourable Company's interest on this side the Continent; but to which I now, with much concern find, it would be ruinous, unless we can fall upon some other practicable route."

After this voyage, Hell's Gate was referred to as the Black Canyon and its rapids were called Simpson's Falls. Now Governor Simpson understood the gravity of the task before him. His voyage and his determination to find "some other practicable route" led to the establishment of Forts Yale and Hope within twenty years.

Economically motivated as they were, travelling and mapping for their employers or for their own purposes, the early explorers and traders made few changes to the land. They built small forts to company specifications using local materials; they bought or hunted local fish and game. They were for the most part interested in exploiting existing resources. They preferred to form alliances with local people and encouraged country marriages between employees and indigenous residents. Traders tended to resist any changes that might have a negative impact on business, which depended upon the plentitude of fur-bearing animals and upon peace among the First Nations. Rivalry between trading companies increased competition for the furs.

Finally, in 1846, the ratification of the Oregon Treaty resolved the territorial dispute. The borderline west of the Rocky Mountains to the Pacific would be extended along the forty-ninth parallel. This new boundary left the Hudson's Bay Company's regional headquarters at Fort Vancouver on the Columbia River in American territory. Chief Factor James Douglas had already begun construction of Fort Victoria on Vancouver Island and after the boundary treaty was signed, he moved the company headquarters to Victoria. In 1849, the Hudson's Bay Company was granted a charter for Vancouver Island. In 1850, Vancouver Island became a colony, and in 1851, Douglas became its Governor. He retained his position as Chief Factor over other unorganized parts of the British-controlled Columbia region, on the mainland, where business had been moved back behind (north of) the new line.

Fort Langley, established along the south bank of the Fraser River in 1827, now became a more important foothold on the mainland. At Fort Langley, a farm provided vegetables, meat, and dairy products. Wooden-staved barrels were built and filled with salmon and berries purchased from First Nations suppliers. A fish processing plant was set up along the Fraser near Chilliwack in 1839. Along with the bales of furs, traded goods were sent back to England or were sent to other forts to feed the employees. Now that access up the Columbia was denied them, Chief Factor Douglas wanted another fort that would get traders as close as possible by river transportation to the long and difficult overland pack trails that the company would be forced to use to reach interior forts.

Hudson's Bay Company employee Alexander Caulfield Anderson was searching for a "practicable route" overland in 1846. He asked the Sto:Lo for assistance. Guides showed him their traditional route, the Silver-Skagit Trail. The easiest access inland from the Fraser Valley is up Silverhope Creek to make the connection with the Skagit River Valley at Kilometre

Forty-two. However, Anderson, sensing they were travelling straight south rather than east, lost faith in his guides and refused to continue. Ironically, Skagit translates as "something hidden" or "the hidden pass." Although it was later proposed as a route for the Hope-Princeton Highway, this access up the Skagit River valley into the Cascades has never been developed beyond the hiking trail it is today.

Anderson recommended that the Company send the brigades over trails up the Fraser Canyon. In 1847, Fort Yale, named for Chief Factor James Murray Yale at Fort Langley, was constructed at the head of navigation on the Fraser. However, the overland route, the Douglas Portage north from Fort Yale, was too difficult. Brigades of packers, with their laden horses and mules, struggled over the mountains north of Yale, crossed the river by ferry north of Spuzzum, climbed Cascade summits over to the Coquihalla Valley, and then trekked north to Merritt and Kamloops. On the first trip, seventy of four hundred animals died, and only fifty of the seventy lost 125-pound packs were retrieved. [Harvey, CC] The route was so difficult that an inexperienced packer committed suicide to avoid scaling the trail again. Extra animals accompanied pack trains to replace those lost in falls along this Brigade Trail. The canyon route to Kamloops was only used for one season.

In 1847, company employee Henry Newsham Peers found a route somewhat easier than the canyon portage. His Brigade Trail went up the Coquihalla River to Peers Creek, over to Sowaqua Creek, and through Fool's Pass to the Tulameen, then north to Kamloops.

An alternate route called the Hope Pass crossed at the headwaters of Whipsaw Creek and went east towards Princeton and the Okanagan Valley. At the spot where Peers' footpath met the Fraser River, the Hudson's Bay Company began construction of Fort Hope in October, 1848. The fort was east of where the cairn stands today, along the waterfront, between Fort and Hudson Bay Streets. Ovid Allard was sent up from Fort Langley to oversee construction. He is said to have named the new fort L'Esperance. Although the company traditionally named its forts after employees, company partners, or members of the royal family, L'Esperance, which translates as Hope, may be an exception. The traders and brigade drovers all hoped for an easier route inland.

To build the fort, part of the flat delta land was cleared of the old growth forest to provide pasturage for the pack animals. The logs from the cut timber were used to construct the stockade and docks, to frame the buildings, to build corrals, and to provide fuel. Fort Hope was open during the busy spring, summer, and fall seasons. For the first few years, when trails were buried in snow during the winters, the traders retreated to Fort Yale. Besides the commemorative street names in Hope townsite, Hudson's Bay Company employees Anderson, Manson, Macleod, Ogilvie, and Peers are remembered in creeks, mountain peaks, or ridges named after them. Alexander Caulfield Anderson named Mount Outram to honour his uncle, Sir James Outram, who served during the Indian Mutiny. William "Dad" Yates, an Orkneyman who came to clerk for the Hudson's Bay Company at Fort Hope in 1854, remained and raised his family in Hope.

Fort Hope remained active for forty-three years, through the gold rush, colonial status, the province-making era, and the first spurt of railroad building. The fort marked a shift in the way humans related to the landscape—a change from "living" in Hope to trying to "make a living." It marked the beginning of European settlement and of the resource-extraction and the transportation industries in the Hope region.

For some years, Fort Hope was administered as an outpost from Fort Yale, where a fire destroyed most records in 1881. When Fort Hope was finally closed in 1892, an official writing to company headquarters implied that this good business decision was long overdue. "It should certainly have been wound up years ago as profitable trade had become impossible." [HBC Archives] By 1892, there were "but six whites left in the village and a few Indians engaged in wood chopping." Sicamous on the Canadian Pacific Railway became the new starting point for pack trains to the Interior. Those heading to the Cariboo set out from Ashcroft.

After the construction of Fort Hope, further exploration fell to prospectors, and to the engineers and surveyors seeking routes for roads and railroads. However, one final explorer is remembered in the rocks of this district. The British had continued to explore the Arctic while searching for the NorthWest Passage to Asia. Sir John Franklin set out from England in the *Erebus* and the *Terror* on May 19, 1845, and never returned. For ten years, the British Admiralty offered a reward to any explorer who could explain the mystery of what happened to Franklin, his ships, and crew. In 1855, the prize was awarded to John Rae who concluded that all had perished on or near King William Island.

Franklin's widow, Lady Jane Griffin Franklin, was not satisfied with this resolution. She refused to give up hope that her husband might still be found. She used her considerable fortune to finance other searches. She travelled the world on public speaking tours to raise money for her obsession. In 1860, while in the northern United States, she heard a report that led her to suspect that news of her husband's fate could be found in northern British Columbia. [Berton, AG] In 1861, with her companion Sophia Cracroft, planning to visit a friend, Captain George Richards, RN, who was in British Columbia with the Boundary Commission, Lady Franklin booked passage around the horn of South America and up the West Coast. [Hill, SREBC]

The English ladies stopped for tea with Governor and Mrs. Douglas in Victoria. From New Westminster, their Royal Engineer hosts arranged passage for them up the Fraser River on the new steamboat service carrying supplies and miners searching for gold. When they reached Yale, they were greeted by local residents who had strung a welcoming banner proclaiming "Lady Franklin Pass." Hudson's Bay Company officials helped Lady Franklin hire canoes to paddle her across the river. At the point beyond which no boat can safely go, where the many-eyed Transformer cramps the current, the outcrop was re-named Lady Franklin Rock in her honour.

ON-GOING CHANGE

"There stumbled a miner fresh from the creeks, dog-dirty, and loaded for bear."

—Robert Service, "The Shooting of Dan McGrew."

On-Going Change

The Fraser River Gold Rush (Wallace & Water)

First Nations people, explorers, and fur traders made few serious alterations to the landscape. The Brigade Trails were no more than footpaths, wide enough for one horse or mule laden with a pack to walk on. The forts themselves, which serviced the fur trade industry, were mere clearings in the wilderness of trees, always adjacent to water transportation, with their backs to the mountains. Food was shipped in, or harvested in the rivers, lakes, and mountains nearby. However, the forts (Yale and Hope) and the Brigade Trails had only been operating for a short ten years before everything changed.

When that First Nations family fishing along a tributary of the Thompson River found a huge gold nugget in the sand in 1857, they took it to the nearest fort to trade it. The Hudson's Bay Company purchased the nugget. Its acquisition was duly recorded in fort ledgers before it was sent out with the company business packets. Word spread from the San Francisco vault that the Hudson's Bay Company was depositing gold. By April 25, 1858, the first prospectors were on the river. Within a year, the Fraser region was flooded with miners feverish for riches. The white population of 150 in New Caledonia, as the British-controlled Columbia region was called, ballooned to as many as ten thousand at any one time. Fresh from the worked-out goldfields of California, the miners were eager to wash the sandbars for nuggets and rock flour of gold.

The Fraser River Gold Rush caught everyone unprepared. In eastern parts of Canada, it had been British policy not to allow immigration and settlement into new land before treaties were negotiated with the First Nations who inhabited the territory. This did not happen in British Columbia. Ten thousand at a time, their population constantly in flux, an estimated thirty thousand uninvited miners arrived. Hudson's Bay Company officials, attempting to keep order, as was their duty under the terms of their Charter, asserted their authority as legitimate representatives of the British Crown in this territory. Chief Factor Douglas forced miners to go through customs as they entered the Fraser River and to purchase a mining permit when they got to Fort Hope, before they could commission a boat ride to the sandbars up river.

Twenty to thirty thousand men tried their luck, turning and turning the bars again, panning sand and gravel or shovelling it down wooden water sluices.

Services such as food, accommodation, travel, and recreation moved in to meet the needs of thousands of men far from their homes. Houses, hotels, bars, an assay office, stores, and laundries sprang up around the fort. Ferries took people across the river; boats were hired to take miners to the workings. New jobs opened up: piloting the steamboats, cutting wood for fuel, logging timber for lumber and cribbing, working in the mill. John Coe's sawmill, the first on the mainland, opened in 1858, on the waterfront near Fort Hope. [Cairnes]

The sawmill was east of the fort, where Old Hope-Princeton Way flares up to join the freeway today. The water lead from the Coquihalla poured through the mill into the Fraser where it bends near Greenwood Island. This island is Indian reserve land, rumoured to be the site of a murder. It is sacred ground; ancient iron-fenced graves are hidden by the trees. Once home to a Great Blue Heron rookery, it has never been developed. Greenwood Island and Bristol Island downstream are typical of landforms that build up at the confluence of creeks and rivers. Sandbars also grow where changes in the current assist deposition along the riverbanks. These placers of the Fraser River, especially Hill's Bar between Hope and Yale, attracted miners here for mainland British Columbia's first gold rush.

Placers are the waterborne or glacial deposits of gravel or sand that contain particles of heavy ore minerals such as gold or platinum eroded from their original bedrock, moved, and dropped. In placer mining, panning and sluicing wash the loose but heavy dust or flour out of the sand. In less than twenty years, Hill's Bar alone yielded $2,000,000 worth of gold. [Lyons]

The gold rush brought the first influx of immigrants to this region. Miners came from all over the world, most funnelled through California. Their numbers included thousands of Chinese labourers who had worked in the California fields. Chinese miners made extra money by shipping British Columbia jade, a semi-precious stone, back home to China where it was prized for carving. Thirteen hundred miners lived in Yale; four hundred lived in Hope, in tent cities that sprang up around the forts. The rest camped on bars and along creeks where their claims were staked. The names of these bars record the variety of origins or the names of the miners who worked them—American, Boston, Chapman, China, Cornish (Murderer's), Emory, Hill, Kanaka (Hawaiian), Sailor, Texas, Union Bar. For a few short years, Yale was the largest city west of the Mississippi and north of San Francisco.

In the frontier boomtown mentality, violence threatened to erupt at any moment. A correspondent writing in June of 1858 from Fort Hope to the *Victoria Weekly Gazette* described the general situation: "I have been here for several days and have seen quite a number of persons from the bars above. From them I learn that there is but little doing in the way of mining; the river is too high, and but few persons are at work. There are about one thousand men here at present. . . . I would advise all that think of coming here to remain where they are at present, for it will be at least six weeks before they can do anything here—perhaps longer. . . . Quite a number are leaving here, cursing the mines. There are but few provisions for sale here. . . . There is great need of an established system of local government here. A gambling house has already opened here; and if the means are not taken to suppress it more will follow. Then, in this period of inaction, drinking and fighting will become the order of the day."

Although Robert T. Smith was appointed the first Justice of the Peace and Revenue Officer at Hope in 1858, and both Yale and Hill's Bar had resident magistrates (Whannell and Perrier, ex-army and ex-navy respectively, but both British subjects), the reporter's observations of impending violence did prove to be prophetic. On Hill's Bar, during Christmas festivities in 1858, Ned McGowan almost instigated war. An incident caused by alcohol abuse and an American who took it upon himself to assault Dickson, a Black citizen of Yale, created an uproar which brought out the Chief Magistrate, the Marines, and a vanguard of Royal Engineers to investigate. However, by then, the authorities were somewhat more prepared; order had been imposed and the show of force sufficed. [The Gold Rush Town of Yale]

The Fraser River Gold Rush did not last long. Within two years, news of new finds farther north attracted most of the gold-seekers to the Cariboo. However, not all of the prospectors were "fly-by-night." Some, such as Henry Hunter, arrived from California for the Fraser River rush and then moved to the Cariboo searching for gold. Hunter returned to the Hope area in 1866.

By this time, Governor Douglas' land policies were in force. All land belonged to the Crown. Applicants could purchase land outright. Alternatively, if they were British subjects, they had the option of pre-empting—claiming a plot of land, usually 160 acres, on the promise that they would improve it. Improvements included clearing the land of virgin forest, building a shelter, settling (or recruiting settlers), and planting an orchard or starting a farm or other business. If the pre-emptor fulfilled obligations within an allotted time, he was awarded the patent for the land for a nominal fee. Hunter pre-empted land where Hunter Creek flows into the Fraser some twelve kilometres west of Hope.

Sidney Herrling of Herrling Island and Billy Bristol of Bristol Island, near where Silverhope Creek enters the Fraser, also arrived as gold-seekers and remained or returned to pre-empt their islands. Andrew Lorenzetto came from Italy via China and California during the Fraser River Gold Rush and later ran a pack train business to the Cariboo before pre-empting along the Fraser. Manuel Alvarez, a Spaniard from Chile who came from California to the Fraser River seeking gold, was another who chose to pre-empt and make a new home here. Jean "Cataline" Caux, a French-born drover who contracted his mule-team to haul Company brigade packets and supplies from Yale to Barkerville along the new Cariboo wagon road, married Amelia, a local woman, and has descendents still living in Yale and Hope. Caux, who moved to the Skeena Valley after railroads destroyed his business in the south, continued to work as a packer until he was too old to ride.

While the gold miners were along the Fraser, they also stumbled upon ruby and garnet crystals and veins of quartz, an indicator mineral often associated with precious metals imbedded in hardrock. Such finds suggested that when the placers were mined out, hardrock mining might be lucrative. Since then, gold dust has been panned; gold nuggets have been picked, and gold veins mined. The search for the motherlode of the gold and platinum, the source from which the dust and rock flour trickled, led eventually to many other discoveries. In 1868, George Shaley registered the first Crown-granted hardrock mine claim in the colony. This is the mine—fifteen kilometres south of Hope, on Silver Peak—with the narrow gauge railway track visible from the second lookout on Landstrom Ridge. On a nearby mountain, the Eureka and Van Bremer mining operation was halted by litigation in 1874 and sat idle for fifty years. In the sixty years between 1860 and 1920, when Hope's population hovered around 200, according to the Geological Survey of Canada [Cairnes], one half of local residents were employed in mining.

After the rush to the Cariboo in the 1860s and before the rush to the Klondike in the 1890s, there was a short-lived mining frenzy in Washington Territory, at Ruby Creek in the Skagit River watershed near the southern tip of Ross Lake. As there was no easy direct route in, prospectors came up the Fraser River to Hope or from Bellingham Bay over the Whatcom Trail to the Skagit

River. Fort Hope sold supplies, and local residents contracted as guides and packers. In 1879, three men from Hope, William Lewis Flood, William Starret, and James Corrigan, headed for Ruby Creek, packing in on Silver-Skagit Trail as far as the Klesilkwa River. There they built a raft that they dubbed "The Steamboat" and the place they launched it they named "Steamboat Landing." The mountain that overlooked the launch site came to be called Steamboat Mountain. The Ruby Creek gold was soon mined out and most of the prospectors left. The area where the placers were located has since been erased from the map; it now lies beneath the waters held back by the Ross Lake Dam.

The mountains of the Skagit and Hozameen ranges continued to attract prospectors. Thirty years after the Ruby Creek rush, two more Americans, Dan Greenwalt and W. A. Stevens, arrived in Hope. As they were buying supplies, they mentioned that they were here to prospect in the Skagit. When helpful local residents informed them that the mountainous region was under several feet of snow and would remain so for some months, the entrepreneurs volunteered that they already knew where they were going to stake their claim. Indeed, they had a map to the gold, given to them by a man on his deathbed, an old prospector who had found it thirty years before. Steamboat Mountain, they said. That was the place.

The secret of their lost mine was out. Even before the trails were free of snow, prospectors and the industries that service them flooded in. Three townsites sprang up around Steamboat Mountain, each with hotels, stores, and restaurants, with houses and tent cities encircling them. There was one assay office and plans for a mill connected by a tram to a mine on the mountain. Within six months, in the spring of 1911, three hundred to five hundred miners were in the area and seven mining companies had been incorporated. Those who were unable to prospect themselves were eager to invest in shares of the Steamboat Mountain gold mine. They had seen the samples Greenwalt and Stevens brought back in their saddlebags. The gold was visible. Who needed an assayer's chemicals and burners to confirm what any fool could see?

It is a story familiar to most mining districts. When something sounds too good to be true, beware. The desire to get rich quickly can become an easily-exploited gullibility. Just before the assay sample was due to return, the mine owners mysteriously left town. The assay results determined the sample to be worthless ore that had been salted. The visible gold used to deceive potential investors was identified as shavings from American coins. By the time the whole story was revealed, Greenwalt and Stevens had left the country with between eighty and ninety thousand 1911 Canadian dollars. The abandoned Steamboat boomtowns left little trace; their timbers were absorbed back into the landscape. When the Skagit watershed was surveyed in 1920 by the Dominion Geological Survey, 2153-metre Steamboat Mountain reverted to its original name, Shawatum.

The Steamboat Mountain swindle did have some positive results. During the year that the rush was on, a road into the Cascades was surveyed and construction began at both ends, including some ten miles up Silverhope Creek. The crash of the mining development and World War I interrupted work on the road and it was never completed. Furthermore, prospectors attracted by the Steamboat project remained and found other workable claims in the mountains encircling Hope. In the Skagit, silver was mined at Silver Daisy south of Sumallo Grove and at the Foundation claim off the Dewdney Trail. In the Hozameen, between 1916 and 1920, prospectors filed the Pipestem claim at the headwaters of Ladner and Siwash Creeks. The Carolin Mine on Ladner Creek was one of several gold mines. Silver was mined at Canim, silver-lead at Summit, and copper at Independence, between Bear Creek and Coldwater River. Across the Fraser River, in the Coast Mountains, Nickelmine Road commemorates the large BC Nickel mine which operated there for years; tailings from the underground mine were sent down the mountain to be stored in a huge, open pit.

Today, rumours of mine re-openings fluctuate with the price of gold. Claims are still staked; mineral exploration is still a common activity. Rockhounds spend happy hours panning the sandbars where men of the Fraser River Gold Rush staked their claims, where Chinese labourers who remained after the railroad was completed re-worked the placers.

The Fraser River Gold Rush thus marked the beginning of another major industry, mining, in the region around Hope. However, back in 1858 when it all began, conflicting cultures and attitudes, alcohol, and gold lust were an explosive mixture. James Douglas, Governor of Vancouver Island and Chief Factor of New Caledonia, recognized the many risks immediately, and moved to try to prevent social and political catastrophe. He quickly formulated a plan to establish and maintain order in the disputed territory.

ON-GOING
CHANGE

"Onward! Christian soldiers, marching as to war."

—S. Baring-Gould

On-Going Change

From Territory to Colony (Christ Church Anglican)

In 1858, the gold-hungry prospector immigrants interfered inevitably with the fur trade. Many boisterous rowdies enjoyed challenging British authority, reminding everyone else of the American doctrine of Manifest Destiny, and suggesting that the region was destined to be a part of the United States. As recently as 1844, American presidential candidate James Polk had run on a platform of "Fifty-four Forty or Fight." The fifty-fourth parallel this slogan refers to was the Russian border. Today it is the southern tip of the Alaskan panhandle, the boundary between the state of Alaska and northern British Columbia. Such aggressive confidence was typical of the attitude of imperial powers in those times. Great Britain too believed that her ways were superior and that all colonized regions were inferior and would only benefit from the introduction of British culture, including the established Anglican Church. Governor and Chief Factor Douglas, through the Secretary of State for Colonial Affairs, Sir Edward Bulwer-Lytton, kept Great Britain fully apprised of the tensions on the mainland. Douglas suggested changes to better demonstrate the authority of the Crown and to ensure that Great Britain would maintain control of the British part of the Columbia region.

Douglas set up customs offices and stopped foreign ships from entering the Fraser. However, his position with the Hudson's Bay Company was seen as a conflict of interest. Finally, on August 2, 1858, Great Britain rescinded the Company's authority and proclaimed colonial status on the mainland. The forts remained as centres for trade, but the Company monopoly was extinguished and its duty to enforce law and order was transferred to others. In November, 1858, Douglas, still Governor of the Colony of Vancouver Island, was appointed Governor of the Colony of British Columbia.

Sir James Douglas, the Father of British Columbia, was another talented man whose vision helped create both Hope and the province. Nicknamed "Black" Douglas, he was a Scots West Indian who had been born at Demerara, in British Guiana, in 1803. Son of a "free coloured woman" and a Scots merchant, he was educated in Lanark. He joined the North West Company in 1815, remaining with the Hudson's Bay Company after amalgamation in 1821. Douglas' wife Amelia, daughter of the Chief Factor Connolly of Fort St. James, was part Cree. It is said that one of the reasons

Douglas was such a strong proponent of British law and order was because of his aversion to the racist attitudes towards all non-whites which many of the miners brought with them. Although Great Britain had abolished slavery in 1833, in 1858, the American Civil War had still not taken place. Washington and Oregon territories were "free" states, but slavery was still legal in at least half of the States of the American Union. As history would soon show, many Americans were willing to die for their right to choose an economic system that permitted humans to own other humans.

Governor Douglas accomplished a great deal in a short time. He set up systems to ensure good governance in the new colony, including mineral, land, and water policies. He appointed the first judge for the colony, Matthew Baillie Begbie, and Robert T. Smith, the first Justice of the Peace and Revenue Officer at Hope. He also appointed J. Peter O'Reilly to record mine and land claims and to mediate mining disputes as Magistrate and Gold Commissioner. Douglas called for a military presence to be sent to the colony as a demonstration of British authority. A vanguard arrived immediately, and a regiment of Royal Engineers under Colonel Richard Clement Moody arrived in Victoria on Christmas Day, 1858. On January 4, 1859, Moody was appointed Commissioner of Land and Public Works and Deputy Governor.

The Royal Engineers were expected to model civilized behaviour to the rowdy Americans, to police the territory, and to set up stabilizing institutions. They designed schools, churches, and bridges. They built

Yale's Church of St. John the Divine, which opened in 1859. They chose and surveyed a site, New Westminster, for the capital city of the new colony. Its location on the north shore of the Fraser River was considered more strategically defensible and its harbour was deep enough for ocean-going ships to dock.

Here in Hope, the Royal Engineers surveyed the old townsite. Using surveying conventions, they chose the highest summit as a spot elevation landmark. Thus, the tip of Mount Ogilvie is centred on the main street, Wallace, which meets the waterfront at a right angle. On May 24, 1859, to celebrate Queen Victoria's birthday, John D. B. Ogilvy, the Hudson's Bay Company trader, climbed this mountain and placed the Union Jack at its peak. [Forging] The Engineers named Wallace Street in honour of Dr. Peter William Wallace, surgeon-in-chief of the Royal Navy Hospital at Esquimalt and the physician on one of the ships that brought them to Victoria. [Forging] Up from the waterfront, one block west of Wallace, Commission Street commemorates another duty an earlier party of Engineers were fulfilling—surveying the Forty-ninth Parallel as part of the International Boundary Commission. One block farther west, between Park and Douglas streets, the Royal Engineers designed and helped build Christ Church Anglican, and participated in its consecration in 1861. This small wood-frame building beneath tall evergreens is still in use today on its original site. The dark varnished wallboards, the exposed trusses effecting a cathedral ceiling, the shimmer of light through rippling hand-made diamonds of glass create an impression of holy space as only old interiors can do. For what is wood but molecules of earth, air, water, and sunlight transformed into tree? What is glass but liquid sand, with air bubbles and waves petrified inside? The red flags of the Royal Engineers which grace the nave somehow seem not incongruous. Back then, church and state, including the military, worked together to create a new, ordered society.

In trying to govern a new colony peopled by seventy thousand First Nations who had not yet signed treaties and by thirty thousand immigrants who were proud citizens of a foreign nation, James Douglas was forced into a reactive position, always trying to catch up with the needs of the population. He was painfully aware of the on-going threat of American influence. If the British could not meet the needs of the new immigrants, someone else surely would, and someone much closer geographically. Thus, Douglas instituted an urgent but expensive road-building campaign to service the gold-seekers and their new communities.

Douglas attempted to settle the issue of Indian land title on the mainland before his own retirement. He had negotiated treaties clarifying land ownership with the indigenous people around Fort Victoria. However, no treaties had been signed in the colony of British Columbia. He may have thought that First Nations would assimilate willingly and that the land question would be solved when they applied for pre-emptions along with other British subjects. [Adams] However, when the Engineers surveyed to what is now Rupert

Street in Hope, they angered the local chief who had been given assurances in September, 1858, that the townsite would not go beyond Coquihalla Street. Within one year of the first rush of immigrants, there were already differences of opinion between colonial officials and First Nations chiefs. In 1864, Douglas directed William McColl, a retired Royal Engineer contracted to survey lands reserved for Indians, to "mark off Indian reserves around all Indian villages, all land cleared and tilled by Indians, and all land claimed by Indians and their heirs. No reserve was to be less than ten acres for each grown man." McColl documented Douglas' direction "to give the Indians as much land as they wished, and in no case to lay off a reserve under one hundred acres."

Unfortunately for the people of British Columbia today, Governor Douglas' successors in provincial politics had neither his vision nor his sense of justice. The Douglas reserves were continually reduced to smaller and smaller parcels that would not support the population attached to them. Nor were the treaties ever negotiated, although the federal government was assured when British Columbia became a province that treaties with the First Nations would be finalized. The issue remains unresolved over one hundred and thirty years later. The entire population of mainland British Columbia west of the Rockies (prior to the Nisga'a Treaty) occupies unceded territory.

Although James Douglas' achievements were considerable, so was the debt incurred by the new colony. New solutions had to be found, as well as new leaders to propose them. Queen Victoria knighted Sir James Douglas the year his governorships ended in 1864. Port Douglas, at the north end of Harrison Lake, the first terminus of the first road to the Cariboo goldfields, was named for him, as was Douglas Street in the newly surveyed town of Hope.

The Royal Engineers were disbanded after five years, in 1863. Besides the surveying, designing, building, and road construction they completed, they also trained colonists to continue the work on their own. "Douglas harnessed the skills of these remarkable military frontiersmen and urged them on to ever greater challenges. . . . the Royal Engineers painstakingly educated the rough and ready colonists in how to build timber cribs and trestles, how to drill and blast rock, and how to build that rock into walls to support their narrow but stable roadways, in areas 'where no sensible roadbuilder should venture.' " [Harvey, CC] Probably their most lasting impact stems from the fact that one officer, Lieutenant Robert Burnaby, and 143 of 158 enlisted men remained in British Columbia as pre-emptors, granted land on the promise that they would improve upon it. They had come to do a job and they stayed to make a new life for themselves, helping to build a nation as they did so.

ON-GOING CHANGE

"And every man's a millionaire if only he can brag
That he was born in Canada beneath the British flag."

—E. Pauline Johnson,
"Canadian Born"
from *Flint and Feather*

On-Going Change

From Colony to Province—Road Links (Ferry Landing)

The Fraser River was the first thoroughfare, its waters linking people living in its lower watershed. First Nations canoe pullers, explorers like Simon Fraser, and traders like George Simpson paddled past the Coquihalla delta. With the gold rush, steamboat service arrived in 1858. There were docks near the fort and ferry landings at the end of Water Street, where the bridge is, and farther up river, at the end of Rupert Street, where the public boat launch is today. Customers could rent small boats or hire boatmen to transport them across the river, or up or downstream to mine locations.

On June 6, 1858, the first paddlewheel steamboat, the S. S. *Surprise*, owned by the California Steam Navigation Company out of San Francisco, docked at the Hope waterfront. The sternwheeler S. S. *Umatilla* was the first to dock at Yale, on July 21, 1858. It was on the steamboats that 116 women arrived between 1862 and 1863. They had been recruited in England and had crossed the ocean in "bride ships" to become wives for prospectors and settlers in the colonies. [Forging] British Columbia's "first tourist," an Englishman named Walter Cheadle, boarded the *S. S. Reliance* at Yale, September 18, 1863, *en route* to New Westminster. He noted in his journal: "We passed Hope, a town of thirty or forty houses, size of Yale, but now 'gone in'. It is most beautifully situated in a large flat with a magnificent amphitheatre of mountains behind. Prettiest site I have seen in the Colony."

However, the prospectors and others servicing their needs required routes to get beyond Lady Franklin Rock and the amphitheatre of mountains surrounding Hope. Under Douglas's direction, the Royal Engineers surveyed the Hope Mountains in anticipation of building a wagon road through the Hozameen Range. Describing the condition of the Hudson's Bay Company brigade pack trails in 1862, Lieutenant Henry Spencer Palmer reported: "slippery, precipitous ascents and descents, fallen logs, overhanging branches, roots, rocks, swamps, turbid pools, and miles of deep mud." [Harvey, CC] Edgar Dewdney and Walter Moberly were awarded the contract to construct the road to the Okanagan. Segments of this Engineers Road begun in 1859 are still visible east of Hope along the Hope-Princeton Highway. However, more gold was discovered farther north in 1860 and the Engineers were re-assigned to work on the road to the Cariboo.

At the same time, private interests were constructing new routes. In 1860, Jonathan Reece, who ran a butcher shop in Yale, pre-empted land around what is now the Five Corners in downtown Chilliwack. To increase his profit, he planned to raise cattle in the valley and drive them to Yale on the hoof. He had been buying cattle in Oregon, transporting them by boat to Bellingham, driving them on the hoof over the Whatcom Trail, and then freighting them by boat to Yale. In order to get his produce to his market, Reece and two helpers macheted, axed, and sawed a footpath from Chilliwack to Yale along the north shore.

In 1860, gold was discovered east along the Forty-ninth Parallel at Rock Creek. Edgar Dewdney was awarded the contract and built the Dewdney Trail, 1.2 metres wide, from Hope to Princeton that same year. Dewdney's future brother-in-law, John Fall Allison, and the citizens of Princeton pushed this trail as far east as Rock Creek. In 1864, Governor Seymour called Dewdney back from the Fraser Canyon and contracted him to extend the Dewdney Trail from Rock Creek to the Kootenays. It reached Galbraith's Ferry on the Kootenay River, near present-day Fort Steele, in 1865.

After British Columbia joined Confederation, James Wardle, Hope merchant, postmaster, and mail carrier, rode this eighteen hundred-kilometre round-trip trail to Fort Steele once a month for years, delivering the Royal Mail under contract for the Government of Canada. Wardle had come from England on the same boat that brought the Royal Engineers in 1858. He worked in the Cariboo for ten years before being awarded the federal mail contract. The mail service would have been impossible if the trail had not already been built. The Dewdney Trail was one of the roads that helped link regions together. The rich mining territory of the interior mountains was susceptible to American influence, ever present and geographically closer than New Westminster or Victoria. Government spending on construction contracts helped bind loyalties; government services helped create community and define identity.

After gold was discovered 650 kilometres north of Hope in 1860, the Royal Engineers were re-assigned to survey a wagon road to the Cariboo. At first, they constructed a wagon road over the trail Governor Douglas had paid unemployed miners to slash the summer before from Port Douglas on the northern tip of Harrison Lake to Lillooet on the Fraser River. Other crews surveyed and began construction from Yale to Barkerville in 1861. Their Cariboo Wagon Road, built by contractors between 1861 and 1864, changed the face of the Fraser Canyon. Using wooden cribbing, the roadbed rested on gangly extensions of grasshopper trestles far out over the chasm, braced against the rocks below. Over its formidable grade, horse-drawn wagons and stagecoaches such as the famous BX (Barnard's Express) could now make the trip to the Cariboo in four days, although mule trains and ox teams still took twenty to thirty days.

The Cariboo Road included the first bridge across the Fraser River, built just north of Spuzzum. The Alexandra Suspension Bridge, named to honour the recently wed Alexandra, Princess of Wales, opened in 1863. It had been designed by the Royal Engineers and built by Joseph Trutch, later the first Lieutenant Governor, who made a fortune on the toll. The tollbridge was washed out by the flood of 1894 and rebuilt by extending the height of the timber footings, but both the road and the bridge had already fallen into disuse by then. The Canadian Pacific Railroad built over several sections of the Cariboo Wagon Road from 1880 to 1885, literally "wiping out" their competition.

Edgar Dewdney had worked on Cariboo Road contracts before being re-deployed to complete the Dewdney Trail. This man too made important contributions to Hope, to British Columbia, and to Canada. Born in 1835, he had come from Devonshire, England with a civil engineering degree. He surveyed New Westminster under contract to the Royal Engineers before taking a fateful steamboat ride up to Hope. On the paddlewheeler, he met his future wife, Jane Shaw Moir, whose stepfather Thomas Glennie farmed along the Coquihalla River, where the Glen-halla Subdivision is now. Jane's mother, Louisa Glennie, opened the first school in Hope in the Anglican manse in the 1860s and was the first public school teacher in 1871. In 1868, Jane's sister, Susan Louisa Moir Glennie, married John Fall Allison, a rancher from Princeton, for whom the Allison Pass is named. On March 28, 1864, Edgar Dewdney and Jane Shaw Moir were the first couple married in Hope's Christ Church Anglican.

Edgar Dewdney, switching careers, moved from engineering into colonial politics. As a cost-cutting measure, the two colonies had been united as one, the colony of British Columbia, in 1866. After Victoria became the capital in 1868, Dewdney was elected to represent Kootenay on the colonial Legislative Council. After British Columbia became a province in 1871, he was elected to Ottawa as Conservative Member of Parliament for Yale in 1872, 1874, and 1878.

Dewdney was Indian Commissioner for the North-West Territories, now Manitoba, Saskatchewan, and Alberta, from 1879 to 1888, the years treaties were being signed with prairie First Nations in anticipation of the railroad crossing the Great Plains. He was also Lieutenant Governor of the North-West Territories from 1881 to 1888 during the years of railroad building and the second Riel Rebellion. In 1888 and 1891 he was re-elected to the House of Commons as Member of Parliament for Assiniboia East. From 1888 to 1892 he held federal cabinet positions as Minister of the Interior and Superintendent of Indian Affairs. He returned to British Columbia as Lieutenant Governor from 1892 to 1897. [TCE]

After an unsuccessful attempt at re-election in 1900, Dewdney retired in Victoria where he worked as a mining broker and financial agent. He continued to consult on engineering projects such as the Kettle Valley Railroad (favouring a route north of the Cascades), the Hope-Princeton Highway, and the draining of Sumas Lake. Dewdney was knighted for his contributions to his nation. In Hope, Dewdney Street commemorates his name. Jane Moir Dewdney pre-deceased her husband. She and her mother, Mrs. Glennie, both died on the same day, in January, 1906, in Victoria. [Titley] Sir Edgar re-married in 1909, and died in Victoria in 1916. In 1920, his widow donated Dewdney's extensive collection of artifacts gathered over a fifty-year career in British Columbia and Canada to the Royal Albert Memorial Museum in Exeter, Devon, England.

After the expense of policing the gold rush and building wagon roads through mountains in the 1860s, Great Britain sought ways to reduce the cost of administering colonies so far from home. It was common knowledge that many Americans believed their nation was destined to rule the North American continent. However, from 1860 to 1865, American armies were fighting each other in a disastrous civil war. Many in Great Britain wondered what would happen when the war ended. Would Americans march on the colonies and territories to the north? Great Britain did not want the additional expense of having to defend distant colonies against American invaders. Colonies in eastern North America were encouraged to unite and to assume more of the responsibilities of governing themselves. Discussions about a Canadian Confederation began as early as 1863. On July 1, 1867, four British North American colonies united. Upper Canada (Ontario), Lower Canada (Quebec), New Brunswick, and Nova Scotia formed the new Dominion of Canada.

After 1867, diplomats in the colonial office were encouraging British Columbia to consider joining Canada. In 1868, citizens of the colony met at the Yale Convention to debate the pros and cons of

149

Confederation. Opinion was in no way unanimous but eventually the colonials decided that it would be in their interest to unite with Canada rather than to choose annexation as an American territory. Pro-Confederation candidates were elected to all seats in the next election. A three-man team, including Sir James Douglas' son-in-law, Dr. Helmcken, travelled to Ottawa to negotiate terms. British Columbia agreed to join Confederation on the condition that Canada would build a railroad to link the West Coast with the east within ten years. The fact that Canada also agreed to cover British Columbia's existing debt helped tip the scales. On July 20, 1871, British Columbia became the sixth province of Canada.

While Prime Minister John A. Macdonald was attempting to raise capital to build the railroad, other more local issues were being dealt with in Hope and in British Columbia. In 1871, Mrs. Glennie opened the first public school in Hope. At the same time, provincial businessmen, still desiring to get meat to market, petitioned the province to survey and construct a road on the south bank of the Fraser. Old Yale Road, built from Ladner to Yale around 1874, is exactly one hundred miles from Ladner to Hope. One of the old milestones, Mile 97, still stands where Tum Tum Road meets Old Yale Road in Silver Creek. A ferry across the Fraser River at Hope linked to the final few miles to Yale. Ladner was the western terminus of Old Yale Road because its harbour, a few miles north of the International Boundary, is a seaport at the mouth of the Fraser. The developers supporting this project, such as John Douglas, founder of the Douglas Lake ranch at Merritt, planned to purchase cattle in the United States, ship them by boat to Ladner, and then save the freight costs by driving them on the hoof to Hope and over the Cascades on cattle trails to Penticton or Merritt. They hoped to reproduce and fatten cattle on the ranchland of the Interior and then drive them back along the same route to be sold to the coastal and American markets. On modern maps, vestiges of Old Yale Road are found in Silver Creek, Rosedale, Chilliwack, Yarrow, Abbotsford, and Langley. It wound around Sumas Lake, which was not drained for another fifty years, in the 1920s.

Old Yale Road was a difficult and costly construction project. At that time in the Fraser Valley, what was not river, lake, marsh grass, or bog land was virgin forest. Road building required cutting through trees, blasting rockfaces, erecting bridges and trestles. The thirty kilometres between Hope and Popkum had twenty-six bridges and numerous timber cribbings. Although it was poorly maintained because of the expense and the depressed economy that followed Confederation, Old Yale Road helped open new territory and thus encouraged settlement in the Fraser Valley. [Harvey, CC] It is because of Old Yale Road that more farms were pre-empted along the Fraser west of Hope such as that owned by William Lewis Flood where Flood Creek flowed into the river.

William Lewis Flood was born in Ontario in 1846. His story is one of many documented in *Forging A New Hope*. Flood and his brother James left home as teenagers intent upon making a fortune. James became a partner in the lucrative Comstock Mine in Nevada, but William moved on to California and then north to British Columbia still seeking the motherlode. He purchased several parcels of land around Fort Hope, including, after the unification of the two colonies, a pre-emption of 160 acres west of the townsite, along what became Old Yale Road. After his venture rafting on the "Steamboat" to Ruby Creek, he returned to work on his properties in Hope. In 1881, he married Susan Suckley, the daughter of an American naval surgeon and a great-granddaughter of Chief Skagit from Kitsap County on Puget Sound. Susan had been educated in Victoria and came to Hope to teach school.

Working from his home in town, William Lewis Flood cleared the giant cedars and firs from his pre-emption. He constructed a sawmill at the mouth of his creek where he transformed the felled trees into lumber that he used in his construction business. He was contracted to build several churches in the Fraser Valley and the extension on to the Onderdonk mansion in Yale, which later became the All Hallows School for Girls. As a sideline of his construction business, Flood also built and sold caskets. In addition, on the cleared land, he planted an orchard and raised livestock. The Floods sold fruit, cider, dairy and meat products locally. Later, after the city grew at the mouth of the Fraser, they sent produce across the river to be shipped by train to Vancouver. After the record high water of 1894, Mr. and Mrs. Flood and their two children moved into a new house on their pre-emption, along the Yale Road, where they were living when the Canadian National Railroad was constructed through their land twenty years later.

The Flood family story is typical of many immigrants then and since. He had arrived in this land with many other speculators, found a beautiful place he wished to live, and worked hard, ever alert for opportunities to supplement his income by recognizing a need and moving to fill a niche. He met the woman he wanted to spend the rest of his life with and together they raised a family. Their name is commemorated today as the Flood district west of Silver Creek, and in the name of the creek and the waterfall. The trailhead from Exit 165 meets Flood Creek below Flood Falls where, a short walk in from the freeway, water tumbles over tiers of plutonic granite in a second-growth forest grotto.

On-Going Change

"Rough quarries, rocks, and hills whose heads touch heaven."

—William Shakespeare, *Othello, the Moor of Venice.*

On-Going Change

Railroads, Highways, and Dams (Fraser River Bridge)

In other parts of Canada, construction on the Canadian Pacific Railroad had begun even before British Columbia joined Confederation in 1871. Contracts were awarded in British Columbia. However, locally, it was almost ten years before residents saw any evidence that a rail line would be a reality. Indeed, when nothing had happened by 1878, the provincial legislature actually took a vote on whether to pull out of Confederation. Finally, American engineer Andrew Onderdonk bought up four contracts to build a railroad from Emory Creek to Lytton. In March, 1880, he moved his headquarters and family to Yale. He was later awarded the final contracts to build the sections west from Emory to Port Moody and east from Kamloops through Eagle Pass to meet the tracks being built from the east.

Although still in his early thirties, Onderdonk had already completed a railroad in South America. He would later build the world's first Ferris wheel, a tunnel under the East River, and New York's first subway. To cut his costs in the Fraser Canyon and to reduce the risk of accidents when transporting explosives, he erected a factory near Emory Creek that manufactured twelve hundred pounds of blasting powder a day. The Powder Magazine stored a large supply of Giant Powder of different grades, while the Chemical works manufactured nitroglycerine. "The Powder Works and Chemical works were twice destroyed by fire and explosions." [Boulet]

Rather than pay the exorbitant freightage to bring in heavy railroad-building supplies over the Cariboo Road, Onderdonk offered reward money to entice steamboat captains to pilot his boat, *The Skuzzy*, through Hell's Gate. The Smith brothers from the Columbia River accepted the challenge. With the aid of towlines and workers pulling from atop the cliffs, the task was accomplished. *The Skuzzy* travelled from Spuzzum to Lytton in two weeks. It worked upriver of Hell's Gate until the CPR railroad was completed. The boat was dismantled and its engine transplanted into a new *Skuzzy* at Kamloops. [Lyons] No steamboat has since attempted the folly of an upriver run through Hell's Gate Canyon.

Onderdonk also brought in six thousand Chinese labourers, some with experience building American railways and some directly from China. Because they could not save enough on their low wages to buy passage home, five thousand settled in Canada after construction was completed. It is said that without their labour, either Onderdonk would have gone bankrupt or Canada would never have acquired a railroad. [Berton, GR] Onderdonk estimated that for every kilometre of track that was laid, three Chinese labourers died. [Woodward, *Land of Dreams*]

The section of the CPR that Onderdonk built north through the Fraser Canyon to meet up with the main line at Kamloops required twenty-seven tunnels and six hundred trestles and bridges across canyons. Rather than attempt to build through the Cascades, the canyon route had been chosen because of its less severe winter conditions. However, the "mountain work" was still a challenge. Cliffs required "incessant blasting. Often huge rocks came hurtling out of the mouths of the tunnels like cannon-balls. . . . The larger blasts touched off avalanches and mud slides. One of these slid down from such a height that it carried part of an oak forest and an entire Indian burying ground into the river, allowing the oaks to continue to grow 'and the dead men's bones to rest without being in the least disturbed—fences, roots, images and all.' " [Berton, GR]

The building of the CPR reflected "a prevalent attitude towards nature at that time." [Boulet] "The right-of-way was literally blasted through the landscape. Nature, as far as railway building was concerned, was an obstacle to the integration of British Columbia with the rest of Canada. . . . scarred, unalterably, but nature would remain a great power to be reckoned with, as every flood, rock slide, avalanche and forest fire insistently made clear."

On November 7, 1885, Donald A. Smith pounded in the last spike of the Canadian Pacific Railroad at Craigellachie in the Rocky Mountains. William Cornelius Van Horne proclaimed "that the work has been done well in every way." Canada was literally a land *a mare usque ad mare,* "from sea to sea." Would technology be able to counter the natural north-south orientation of the mountain valleys and seacoast west of the Rockies, the isolation created by distance and topography that separates British Columbia from the eastern regions of the continent? Would progress be able to tame and civilize nature? If so, at what costs?

The land around Hope was changing—from First Nations ancestral territory, to unexplored country, to trade monopoly, to overrun frontier gold field, to orderly colony with legislative council, to province of a far Dominion. Seven years after the railroad opened, Fort Hope closed and the townsite almost emptied. Thousands of unemployed construction workers had already moved elsewhere. Steamboat service was no longer required, and because the Cariboo Road had been ruined by the railroad-builders, the packers like Jean Caux and the freight companies like Barnard's Express moved their depots north to Ashcroft. Just as an economic depression followed Confederation, another followed the end of railroad construction.

However, back east, the federal government was initiating a plan to keep the railroad busy transporting new residents to the empty territories and new provinces. Advertising and promotion campaigns began all across Europe, offering free land to hard workers. All you had to do was break the sod, plant crops, and build a house for your family, and the homestead would be yours. Recognizing the Government of Canada's offer as the only way they would likely become landowners, thousands of people from around the globe accepted the challenge. They arrived by boat at Halifax or Quebec City or Montreal and, after quarantine, embarked on a train for points west. Some travelled across the prairies and through the mountains to take up land in British Columbia. Immigrant settlers arrived at the station and began pre-empting land around Hope early in the twentieth century.

One such adventurer, Thomas Lindsay Thacker, moved from England and began to build a cabin on a pre-emption of land atop Thacker Mountain in 1904. This is the little mountain with the tower on top, beneath Ogilvie's peak, with the trailhead at the end of Thacker Mountain Road. Mr. Thacker's fiancée joined him to inspect the property in 1906; they married and raised a family there on their mountain. When he died in 1961, Mr. Thacker willed his land to the University of British Columbia. Thacker Marsh along Union Bar Road, an old river course, a glacier path, the route the Kettle Valley Railroad took between the river and the canyon, and a former booming ground for a local sawmill, is now a wetlands ecological reserve developed by the Fraser Valley Regional District. The marsh teems with plant and animal life—water lilies, wild flag, rushes, clams, crayfish, frogs, red-winged blackbirds, ouzels, coyote, wolf, deer, raccoon, lynx, cougar, and bear.

The face of Hope continued to change in the early twentieth century. New immigrants raised young families on new pre-emptions. Between 1901 and 1911, the population of the province more than doubled— from 179,000 to 394,000. The provincial government promised roads to the Interior. Surveys were completed and a route chosen up Silver Creek, over the Skagit Valley, through Lightning Creek Pass, an area where mining exploration was at a peak around Steamboat Mountain. Construction began at both ends, but was interrupted by the war and never resumed. Although subject to "debris torrents, mudslides, and avalanches," [Harvey, CC] this route through the Cascades would have avoided the Skagit Bluffs.

This early twentieth century was an era when people still had faith in technology. If one railroad had brought jobs, immigrants, markets, and trade, two railroads would bring more. Another line would undercut the CPR monopoly. Competition would be good for business. On the left bank of the Fraser River, the east and south side, the Canadian Great Northern Railroad pushed through a second railbed. However, times had changed. Construction was plagued with work stoppages. In March, 1912, workers walked out to protest the dangerous conditions, hours of work, and wages. By April 2, eight thousand men were on strike. Industrial Workers of the World poet and organizer Joe Hill visited the camp at Yale. In an attempt to bolster morale, he wrote several songs, including "Where the Fraser River Flows." This was a new century; workers were no longer willing to sacrifice themselves for someone else's benefit. Strikes were one of the few actions available to them. "The federal government refused arbitration . . . the provincial government broke the strikes with violence and arrests: . . . but the strikes are more important for showing that unskilled workers could be successfully organized." [TCE]

In 1913, after construction had resumed, blasting caused the rock fall that obstructed the already congested Hell's Gate Canyon. A second fall the next spring decimated the salmon run, blocking their return. These trials were omens for the new railroad. The Canadian Northern did not make a profit. By 1919, it was included in a massive federal government nationalization scheme as part of the people-owned Canadian National Railroad. The CNR still runs through Hope; the train stops at the old station site, behind Fifth Avenue and Hudson Bay Street. In an attempt to preserve one of the few heritage buildings in Hope, the original stationhouse was moved to the junction of Old Hope-Princeton Way and Water Avenue.

The strike and the manmade disaster at Hell's Gate did not deter further construction projects. With the increased popularity of private automobiles, road travel came back into vogue. The first bridge to cross the Fraser River at Hope opened in 1915. Still in use today, it was constructed with the cooperation of the provincial government and private enterprise. Premier

Richard McBride envisioned an all-Canadian road route to the east, and the CPR required a link between the Kettle Valley Railroad and the CPR mainline. The CPR Hope Station, which was re-named Haig Station in 1919 to honour a World War I leader, is on the far side of the river. CPR trains of the Kettle Valley line crossed on the lower level of the bridge. Road traffic used the upper level. The bridge, which replaced the ferry, was upgraded in 1949 and in 1996, but its original two-tiered structure remains. In 1999, the Fraser River Bridge was re-dedicated as the Bill Hartley Fraser-Hope Bridge to honour the former Minister of Public Works who represented the constituency of Yale-Lillooet in the provincial legislature from 1963 to 1975.

The bridge across the Fraser was a boon to the town of Hope although for a few years it was "the bridge to nowhere." Cars would drive to the end of the road, up to Hope, where they would be loaded on to flatcars to be freighted by rail over the Cascades. In 1926, the Alexandra Bridge north of Spuzzum was replaced and an early section of the Trans-Canada Highway, incorporating parts of the old Cariboo Wagon Road, was built through the Fraser Canyon. Opened in 1927, the Trans-Canada Highway crossed the Fraser at Hope and followed parts of Old Yale Road down the south shore through the valley to Vancouver. The road through the canyon was a toll highway, with the first tollbooth at Alexandra Bridge. Toll collection moved to Yale from 1937 to 1947. This first historic highway linking east to west across Canada followed the example of the railroads and used the Thompson River valley through Kamloops, thus avoiding the formidable Cascade Mountains.

On the north shore of the Fraser River, Reece's cattle trail became Highway #7, known both as the Haig Highway and also as the Lougheed Highway after Nelson Seymour Lougheed, who attended school in Hope when his father worked for the CPR in the 1890s. Lougheed was appointed Minister of Public Works in 1928. Highway #7 begins or ends at Hope, at the far side of the bridge, where it joins #1, which continues up the canyon through Yale and Spuzzum, past Hell's Gate, Boston Bar, Lytton, to Cache Creek where it turns east to Kamloops. The road north to the Cariboo is now #97 to Prince George.

The present bridge that crosses the Fraser on Highway #1 at Spuzzum opened in 1962, the year Roger's Pass through the Rocky Mountains made the Trans-Canada Highway a reality. The old Alexandra Bridge is still accessible as a provincial recreation area. It offers spectacular views of the Fraser as well as access to remnants of the old Cariboo Wagon Road on the right bank. Bridges and tunnels are links, places where human re-writing, human alteration of unscarred landscape, is most challenged by the traces of cosmic energy written in rock, washed by rushing water.

The wondrous Kettle Valley Railway, built between 1910 and 1919, from Midway in the West Kootenay/ Boundary Country to Hope, was the first to challenge the Cascade Mountains. Sir Edgar Dewdney was commissioned to survey the Hope Mountains in 1901. He suggested three possible passes while expressing a personal preference for a northern route that skirted the Cascades. [Harvey, CWP] Pushed by fear of American competition in the rich Kootenay mining region, the CPR contracted Andrew McCulloch to survey a railroad that most people considered impossible.

McCulloch, an American with a passion for Shakespeare, regaled his men around work camp fires at night with recitations from the bard and travelled at every opportunity to Seattle to attend performances of the plays. The spectacular geology of the Coquihalla Canyon reminded him of a quotation from one of his favourites, *Othello, Moor of Venice:* "Rough quarries, rocks, and hills whose heads touch heaven." [I, iii] McCulloch named his remarkable engineering achievement the Othello Quintette Tunnels. Other station stops in the Coquihalla Subdivision he named for other characters from plays—Jessica, Juliet, Ophelia, Portia, Romeo, Falstaff, Iago, Lear, and Shylock.

Only an engineer with a poet's heart can appreciate the beauty of the landscapes of Hope. To builders, rocks are barriers and destructive blasting is constructive. The poet recognizes the soul in the cedar, stones as sacred vessels, the shaggy sea of mountains as stairways to the sky. Nevertheless, the skills of men like McCulloch, the paths they forge, the constructs they erect, make it possible for others to enter the virgin terrain, to encounter the full glory, or the full fury, if the season shifts, of the places the engineers open, the portals they unlock.

Through high mountain passes threatened by heavy

snowfalls, over wide dry gulches from which glaciers had only recently retreated, across gullies and river canyons, beneath avalanche tracks, on soft unstable metamorphosed sedimentary rock that would not sit still, through hard igneous rock that would not be penetrated, across both the Coquihalla River and the mighty Fraser here in Hope, McCulloch built the KVR. On this line too, construction started from both ends. The two ends met twenty-five kilometres northeast of Hope, at Ladner Creek.

Ladner Creek posed its own problems—a long curved trestle bridge over the creek entered a tunnel through the cliff. However, here, the matrix was not granite as it was at the Othello Tunnels in the Coquihalla Canyon. At Ladner Creek, the old crumbly metamorphosed sandstone of the sediments deposited at the continent's edge defied the technology of the day. A rockfall wiped out the work camp in 1915 and delayed the official opening of the line by one year. That winter, 20.4 metres of snow fell in the Coquihalla Pass, which, on average, receives twice the precipitation that Allison Pass does, and five times that of the Fraser Canyon. [Harvey, CC]

Hope became a busy terminus for the Kettle Valley Railroad. Automobiles from the coast drove up and were loaded as freight upon the train for the trip across the Hope Mountains. With station stops for two other railroads and the first bridge across the Fraser east of Vancouver, Hope had become a transportation hub again, gateway to the Interior. The settlement was incorporated as a village in 1929. The population reached two hundred by 1920 and 374 in 1931.

The KVR was intended to bring ore and agricultural products from the Kootenays and the Okanagan to the Coast but one of its first sad duties was to carry soldiers to depot during World War I. Fifty-five thousand British Columbians volunteered to fight in France. Some of these young men were from Hope. A brass bookstand in the sanctuary of Christ Church Anglican is inscribed: "In Loving Memory of Pte. Arthur C. Wardle, 47th Batt. N. Fell in Action in France, May 6, 1917, Aged 19 years."

During the 1920s, the KVR helped settlers move into the southern Interior. However, the Stock Market Crash of 1929 and the ensuing World Depression reached this region as well. By the 1930s, forty thousand people were on assistance in Vancouver. Large numbers of unemployed men were sent from the cities to government-sponsored work camps. At least four of these camps were established east of Hope, several more up the Fraser Canyon, and others around Laidlaw and up Jones Lake Road. At the depths of the Depression, more than seven thousand men worked in camps nearby, which, for three years, were administered and supervised by the federal Department of National Defense because the unemployed were considered a potential threat to national security. For pennies more than room and board, relief camp workers pounded rocks with hammers and picks for labour-intensive road building through the mountains.

A highway from Hope to Princeton had been talked about since gold rush days. Work had commenced before 1914 but never resumed after World War I. A new survey through Allison Pass was completed in 1922 and, although promises were made, nothing materialized. In 1929, a government official stated that the work would begin in 1930 and would be completed by 1932, but fate intervened. The project acquired the nickname "the Great Procrastination." In 1933, the province made the decision to "use the high line in the upper Skagit Valley" rather than the valley floor route, but nothing was done until 1938. [Harvey, CC]

During World War II, the work relief camp at Sunshine Valley was transformed into the Japanese Internment Camp called Tashme. Thirty-six hundred internees lived there. [Anderson, *70 Places*] Some of the men continued to work on road building. The gates to Hope were unlocked after the war, although full civil rights for people from the internment camps were not restored until 1949.

World War II ended the Depression. However, except for the construction work done by internees, major road building was limited to defensive projects such as the Alaska Highway. Another survey through the Cascades was completed in 1944 and the contracts to build the highway from Hope to Princeton were let in 1946. Part of the route was awarded to Emil Anderson Construction Company from Thunder Bay, Ontario. The company moved its headquarters to Hope. On November 2, 1949, the Hope-Princeton Highway was opened.

The competition between roads and rails continued. The Hope-Princeton provided access to the Okanagan and the Kootenays. Trucks and buses using the Hope-Princeton Highway competed for rail passengers and freight. The KVR became less important. Today, the steep trail to the Ladner Creek trestle on the old Kettle Valley Railway climbs over the tunnel, which is blocked again by fallen debris. In 1930, the KVR became a subdivision of the CPR and its Hope terminus was closed. The CPR's KVR Coquihalla Subdivision closed in 1961 and the tracks were removed. It had been active for forty-six years, but proved in the end to be "unmaintainable at a reasonable cost." [Harvey, CWP] Winter conditions were always a problem. Forest fires and ice jams also wreaked havoc on the trestles, and one dry summer, a plague of grasshoppers greased the rails. High costs and washouts finally forced the closure. The rest of the line closed in 1964, pulling up its track too as it left. However, the railbeds are still visible on the faces of cliffs and along valley floors. In many places, hiking trails, including parts of the Trans-Canada Trail, follow the old route—a return to a simpler way, foot and hoof to ground.

In town, the imprint of the Kettle Valley Railroad is still here. At the east end of the double-decker bridge across the Fraser River, where it abuts Hope Street, the old KVR stationhouse is gone but the stationmaster's house is still in use as a private home on its original site. In town, between Hope Street and Kawkawa Lake Road, there are many angled intersections. The track has been pulled up, but the right of way is still visible in the offset streets that bordered it, and in the many triangular-shaped lots that flanked the right-of-way.

Where the CNR tracks cross Sixth Avenue, a footpath leads to Fort Street and to River Parade where the dyke incorporates part of the old railbed.

Across the Coquihalla River, a few steps upstream from the Sucker Creek Salmon Enhancement viewing platforms, the concrete abutment stamped with 1914 is where the KVR bridge crossed the Coquihalla River. The walk through Thacker Marsh on the Trans-Canada Trail follows the old railbed. Across Kawkawa Lake Road, past the gravel pit of the old glacial moraine, at the end of Kettle Valley Road, the trail continues along the grade to the Othello Tunnels.

There are no old engines or railcars or cabooses, but in the tunnels, the ghosts of steel and steam live in the rock. The bluffs and crags of the granite canyon, the water-washed stones of the gorge, are no more awe-inspiring than the engineering marvel of the tunnels, portals into the womb of the mountain. Enveloped in the cool breath of darkness, visitors duck the drips and skip the trickle of water puddling where ties and steel rails once lay.

The tunnels can also be accessed from the Coquihalla Highway, the Othello Tunnels Coquihalla Canyon Provincial Park Exit. The Coquihalla Highway follows the river through the pass, over the Plutonic Belt of the Hozameen Range, through the tollbooths, onto the high dry Interior Plateau, to Merritt. Opened in 1986, in time to bring traffic from the east to Expo '86 in Vancouver, this newest land route linking the Interior and the Coast follows much of the old railroad

Coquihalla Subdivision which in turn had followed the valley corridor through the Hope Mountains.

Along the Coquihalla Highway, signs mark the old station stops. Hiking trails, such as the one to the Ladner Creek tunnel and trestle, lead into the hills. The 115 kilometre section of highway between Hope and Merritt includes "thirty-eight overpasses, a three hundred metre snow shed and many other avalanche control installations, a steelhead fishery diversion," [TCE] and innovative wildlife passages to assure that animals can range without being blocked or killed at the freeway. The section from Merritt to Kamloops opened in 1987 and the connector from Merritt to Kelowna in 1990. In 2000, the Coquihalla was added to the Yellowhead Route and Hope became the western terminus of this third trans-provincial highway, which adjoins the Trans-Canada west of Portage la Prairie, Manitoba.

Railroads and highways were not the only construction projects to wrestle with the mountains. As early as 1906 to 1910, Seattle City Light began eyeing hydroelectric potential on the Washington State side of the Skagit River. In mountainous regions, the force of gravity, of the natural fall of water, can be harnessed to spin turbines that transform the energy into electricity. From its headwaters in Manning Park, the Skagit River flows 240 kilometres southwest to Puget Sound. Three dams, the Gorge High Dam completed in 1924, the Diablo (1936), and the Ross (1952), harness the water's energy to generate power for Seattle. The Ross Lake Reservoir, built precisely in the V where the

Ross Lake Fault meets the Fraser-Straight Creek Fault Line, backs up water for forty kilometres in Ross Lake, which straddles the International Boundary, lapping into British Columbia at times of high water.

Seattle City Light had planned to expand by building a fourth dam, the High Ross. The project would have raised the water level another forty metres and immersed up to five thousand acres in British Columbia. The proposed higher floodplain was logged prior to construction. The Silver Skagit Logging Company, whose base camp was in Silver Creek, across the river from Landstrom Ridge, is estimated to have hauled out a million board feet of logs per day. [Lyons] Eventually, conservation efforts such as those by the Run Out Skagit Spoilers committee and logger-turned-environmentalist Wilfrid (Curley) Chittenden put a stop to the dam expansion plans. In 1984, BC Hydro committed to provide power to Seattle from other sources, mainly in the Columbia River watershed, in return for not raising the water levels in the Skagit Valley. The wilderness area was saved from a permanent man made flood. An international endowment fund was created "to preserve and protect wilderness and wildlife habitat" and "to enhance recreation opportunities."

On the Canadian side of the border, the Skagit Valley Provincial Park and Manning Provincial Park help ensure the preservation of the watershed and conservation of the Skagit Range. On the American side, the land is designated wilderness. The United States National Park Service manages the Ross Lake

National Recreation Area and the North Cascades National Park, where parts of *The Deer Hunter* were filmed in the 1970s. The area has also been immortalized by two American writers, Jack Kerouac and Gary Snyder, who both worked as forest fire lookouts in cabins above Ross Lake. Many of Snyder's poems in *Riprap & Cold Mountain Poems* celebrate Cascade sites; his *Mountains and Rivers Without End* connects philosophically and aesthetically the North American cordillera with the art of the Orient.

Jack Kerouac's *The Dharma Bums* and *Desolation Angels* were inspired by his weeks stationed atop Desolation Peak watching the play of rain, fire, and light. "Hozomeen, Hozomeen, the most mournful mountain I ever seen," his narrator, Ray, chants. Ray takes that job for many different reasons, but by the time his term is up, he has found enlightenment. "I didn't know anything any more, I didn't care, and it didn't matter, and suddenly I felt really free." After watching a storm's show of snow and lightning, Ray steps outside his cabin door and into a rainbow, "a lovely haloed mystery making me want to pray." [Kerouac, DB]

The Ross Lake Reservoir and the International Boundary are sixty kilometres south from Hope up Silver-Skagit Road. BC Hydro's Wahleach Dam on Jones Lake is west of Hope, up a rough road that leaves the freeway at Exit 153. (As the exit numbers measure kilometres from Horseshoe Bay, Exit 153 is seventeen kilometres west of Exit 170.) Wahleach, meaning "its back covered with willows," is the Halkomelem name for the little island in the Fraser River where the creek comes down from Wahleach Lake. In the early 1950s, trees around Wahleach Lake were logged before a dam was built to create the Jones Lake Reservoir that collects rainwater and glacial meltwater from the surrounding Cascade peaks. The drowned tree stumps were removed some forty-five years later.

Water from the Jones Lake Reservoir, which is diverted via a tunnel and penstock (tube) through Four Brothers Mountain, falls a height of six hundred metres from the lake to the Wahleach Powerhouse along the highway, near river level. When the penstock was dug up after forty-five years to be maintained, the metal pipe was found to have bent inside the rock. The theory? Glacial rebound—the land is still rising, springing back after the depression caused by glaciers. This rebound had not been allowed for during construction and had bent the metal pipe as the mountain moved.

Although both Ross Lake and Jones Lake incorporate recreational facilities around their shores, attitudes towards such projects as damming the Skagit River or flooding Wahleach Lake or draining Sumas Lake in the early twentieth century would be very different today. Science has discovered more about how salmon migrate high up into rivers, streams, and creeks to spawn. The public has a greater awareness of the benefits of bogs and wetlands for the fish and wildfowl that need them as breeding places. To prevent industry from destroying the future legacy of the natural world in order to chase the dollar today, logging roads are to be decommissioned, streams left shaded and unclogged. Heli-logging saves many hillsides from bulldozers and the erosion that follows denuding. Environmental impact studies are required if more pipelines, hydro transmission lines, or new industries choose to locate in the region.

With today's greater appreciation of values other than economic, society is less accepting of the old Judeo-Christian assertion that the Earth was created for humankind to dominate. The needs of human populations who choose to move into the watersheds are balanced with the ability of the environment to sustain itself. Recreational, aesthetic, and spiritual values, not to mention First Nations land claims, are to be factored in whenever land-use decisions are made. "The Earth does not belong to man; man belongs to the Earth," as the Elders say.

In 1992, the town of Hope and outlying communities amalgamated as a municipality called the District of Hope. The population, which has always fluctuated as the community cycled through trading-post days, the boom and bust of a gold rush, the construction of three wagon roads, three railroads, and four highways, has settled at under ten thousand. While many pass through, and many make short stops, other people from every continent come to live in the beauty that is here. Whether they have chosen to move here or have been born here and choose to stay, residents work in traditional industries, providing services, transporting people and goods over, around, and through the mountains, extracting resources or timber from them.

Besides the precious metals that have been excavated since the gold rush, industrial materials such as antimony have been mined. Talc deposits are being explored for possible use in paper production. Talc was deposited originally in bent layers or lenses on the ocean floor. When the oceanic plate subducted beneath the continental plate, the talc deposits separated from the oceanic plate and were picked up or abducted to the landmass. Then they were squeezed by intrusions and metamorphosed into a new rock.

Serpentine, which is abundant in the mountains, is valued as a decorative rock and as a stone for carving. White "soda granite" along the contact zone with serpentine is an indicator rock for nephrite jade. Limestone, clay, slate, coal, marble, sand, and gravel have all been quarried nearby. Granite is blasted and trucked to creeks and riverbeds to be used as riprap or to highway construction sites to be used as ballast or fill. Other granite is used as a building stone, for monuments, and in landscaping. Prospectors check out quartz outcrops or interesting patterns such as the spider quartz found near gold veins. Down at the water, panners still wash the sand for gold flecks. Rockhounds scour the shorelines and beaches for newly deposited nuggets, jade, jasper, agate, or other interesting lapidary specimens, thrilling at the variety and colour and complexity of the bits of mountains that have moved downstream to become the river's cobble.

THE GARDEN

"Days and months slip by like water,
Time is like sparks knocked off flint.
Go ahead and let the world change—
I'm happy to sit among these cliffs."

—Han-shan,
Circa 650 to 700 CE,
Cold Mountain poem #17,
translated by Gary Snyder,
in *Riprap & Cold Mountain Poems.*

The Garden

Hope is a place of turmoil and transition, of edges, endings, and beginnings. Every ridge and ripple can be read. With each story the stones have to tell, the waves of mountains become not a challenge but a gift. The rocks continue to attract and to sustain, to move the seekers who step into the flow. A pebble or cobble winks. How was it created? Where did it come from? What waters have borne it? Where will it go from here?

Like stones in the brook of time, or pilgrims, worn and silent, we arrive. Everyone comes to Hope for a reason, seeking relaxation and re-creation, or looking for something, the answer to some question. We walk old trails, step through portals into forest or mountain, climb to the sky, kneel to ground. Sometimes what we find surprises us. Sometimes, it is simply a matter of getting the question right.

Sole to ground, in woodland glade or subtle garden, soothed by the trickle of water on granite, we lift our gaze to the hills. Seeing with new eyes the ancient story of Earth's creation and on-going transformation, of our humble place within it, we re-affirm our connection with the Earth to which we belong.

HERE IN HOPE

RESOURCES AND SOURCES

GEOLOGY RESOURCES

Alt, David D. & Hyndman, Donald W. *Northwest Exposures: A Geologic Story of the Northwest*. Mountain Press. 1995.

_____. *Roadside Geology of Washington*. Mountain Press. 1984.

Bird, J. Brian. *The Natural Landscapes of Canada: A Study in Regional Earth Science*. Wiley. 1980.

Boyer, Davis S. "The Skagit." *National Geographic* 152:1, July, 1977.

Cairnes, C. E. Geological Survey Memoir 119. Coquihalla Area, B.C. Canada Department of Mines. 1924.

Cannings, Sydney & Cannings, Richard. *British Columbia: A Natural History*. 1995?

_____. *Geology of British Columbia: A Journey Through Time*. Greystone. Douglas & McIntyre. Vancouver. 1999.

Clague, John. On the Hope Slide and the Fraser River. E-mail. 1998.

Clague, John J. & Shilts, William W. "Two landslide-dammed lakes in the Cascade Mountains, Southwestern British Columbia." *Current Research*, Part E; Geological Survey of Canada, Paper 93 - IE, p. 47-54.

Doyle, Robert, "Rivers Wild and Pure: A Priceless Legacy." *National Geographic* 152:1, July, 1977.

Eisbacher, Dr. Gerhard H. *Vancouver Geology: A Short Guide*. Geological Association of Canada. 1973.

Foster, Robert J. *Geology*. Charles E. Merrill. 1966.

Goff, Dr. James R. and Hicock, Dr. Stephen R. "Geohazard Risk Assessment of the Klesilkwa Drainage Basin." Paper prepared for the Skagit Environmental Endowment Commission. 1993.

Gore, Rick. "Our Restless Planet Earth." *National Geographic* 168:2. August, 1985. Pages 142-181.

Gunn, Angus. M. *Minerals in British Columbia*. Province of BC Ministry of Mines and Petroleum Resources. Nd.

Hyndman, R. D., *et al.* "Giant Earthquakes Beneath Canada's West Coast." *Geoscience Canada* Volume 23, Number

2, pages 63 - 72. Geological Survey of Canada Publication No. 31095. 1996.

Journeay, J. M. & Monger, J. W. H. *Interactive Geoscience Library: Volume 1.* CD-ROM. Coast and Intermontane Belts of Southwestern British Columbia. Geological Survey of Canada. Open File 3276. Nd.

Longwell & Flint. *Introduction to Physical Geology.* Wiley. 1965.

Mackenzie, Ian. *Ancient Landscapes of British Columbia.* Lone Pine. 1995.

Pearl, Richard M. *How To Know the Minerals and Rocks.* Signet. 1955.

Plummer, McGeary, & Carlson. *Physical Geology.* WCB/ McGraw-Hill. 1999.

Rhodes, Frank H. T. et al. *Fossils: A Guide to Prehistoric Life.* Golden. 1962.

Thurber et al. *Exploring Earth Science Geology.* Allyn and Bacon, Inc. 1976.

U. S. Department of the Interior, National Park Service. *North Cascades: Official National Park Handbook.* 1986.

_____. *Draft General Management Plan and Environmental Assessment.* North

Cascades National Park. Ross Lake National Recreation Area. Lake Chelan National Recreation Area. 1987.

_____. *Chert Procurement in the Upper Skagit River Valley.* Robert R. Mierendorf. 1993.

Yorath, C. J. *Where Terranes Collide.* Orca. 1990.

Zim, Herbert S. & Shaffer, Paul R. *Rocks and Minerals.* Golden. 1957.

Geology Internet Sites: Amethyst Gallery; Canadian Rockhound Magazine; Geological Survey of Canada; Mine-Engineer; Natural Resources Canada; National Park Service, North Cascades National Park and Ross Lake National Recreation Area; Simon Fraser University, Department of Earth Sciences; US Geological Survey; University of British Columbia Earth and Ocean Sciences.

HISTORY RESOURCES

Adams, John. *Old Square-Toes and His Lady: The Life of James and Amelia Douglas*. Horsdal & Schubert. 2001.

Akrigg, G.P.V. & Helen B. *British Columbia Place Names*. Sono Nis. 1986.

Allison, Susan L. "Allison Pass Memoirs." *Canada West Magazine* I:4. Winter, 1969. Pages 25-28.

Anderson, Frank W. Frontier Guide to *The Dewdney Trail Rock Creek to Salmo*. Frontier. 1969.

_____. *The Hope Slide*. Frontier. 1965.

_____. *70 Interesting Places In Southern British Columbia*. Gopher. 1985.

Barlee, N. L. "How to Pan for Gold." *Canada West Magazine* I:1. Spring 1969. Pages 18-23.

Beautiful British Columbia Magazine. *The Fraser River. British Columbia, Canada*. 1983?

Berton, Pierre. *The Arctic Grail: The Quest for the Northwest Passage and the North Pole 1818-1909*. McClelland & Stewart. 1988.

_____. *The Great Railway. Illustrated*. McClelland & Stewart. 1972.

Boulet, Roger H. *Onderdonk's Way*. Kamloops Art Gallery Internet Site. 1997.

Boston Bar-North Bend Enhancement Society. *The Canyon Then and Now*. 1996.

Bouvette, W. S. *The True Story of the Cariboo Wagon Road*. Np/nd.

BC Hydro Brochure. Jones Lake Reservoir Recreation Area.

BC Parks Brochures. Coquihalla Canyon Recreation Area. Manning Provincial Park. Skagit Valley Recreation Area.

British Columbia Centennial '71 Committee. *It Happened in British Columbia*. 1971.

The Canadian Encyclopedia Plus, 1996. [TCE] James Marsh, Editor. CD-ROM. McClelland and Stewart. 1995.

Cheadle, Walter B. *Cheadle's Journal of Trip Across Canada 1862 - 1863*. Hurtig. 1971.

Dahl, Ervin. *Gateway to the Interior: A Brief History of Hope*.

Chilliwack. 1971.

Doeksen, Gerry. *Kettle Valley Railway: Railways of Western Canada. Volume One.* Montrose. 1981.

Drucker, Philip. *Indians of the Northwest Coast.* The American Museum of Natural History. 1955.

Fraser, Simon. (Lamb, W. Kaye, ed.) *The Letters and Journals of Simon Fraser 1806-1808.* Macmillan. 1960.

Geddes, Gary (ed.) *Skookum Wawa: Writings of the Canadian Northwest.* Oxford. 1975.

Glavin, Terry. *This Ragged Land.* New Star. 1997.

Grant, The Revd. George M. *Ocean to Ocean: Sandford Fleming's Expedition Through Canada in 1872.* "From Kamloops to the Sea." James Campbell & Son, Toronto. 1873.

Haig-Brown, Allan and Blackclaws, Rick. *The Fraser River.* Harbour. 1996.

Harvey, R. G. *Carving the Western Path: By River, Rail, and Road Through B.C.'s Southern Mountains.* [Harvey, CWP] Heritage House. 1998.

_____. *The Coast Connection.* [Harvey, CC] Oolichan. 1994.

Hill, Beth. *Exploring the Kettle Valley Railway By Car, Foot, Skis, Horseback or Mountain Bike.* Polestar. 1989.

_____. *Sappers: The Royal Engineers in British Columbia.* Horsdal & Schubart. 1987.

Hofstadter, Miller & Aaron. *The United States: The History of a Republic.* Prentice-Hall, Inc. 1957.

Hope/Fraser Canyon Community Development Society. *District of Hope and the Fraser Canyon Community Profile.* 1995.

Hope and District Chamber of Commerce. *Hope Daytripper's Paradise.* Annual.

Hope and District Historical Society. *Forging a New Hope, Struggles and Dreams, 1848-1948: A Pioneer Story of Hope, Flood, and Laidlaw.* [Forging] Hope. 1984.

The Hope Standard.

Hudson's Bay Company Archives. *Fort Hope Information Package.* 1997.

Hunter, Don. "Ex-logger fought to save woods." *The Province,* 95.10.03, p. A34.

Hutchison, Bruce. *The Fraser.* Clarke Irvin. 1950.

Loo, Tina. *Making Law, Order, and Authority in British Columbia, 1821-1871.* University of Toronto. 1994.

Lyons, C. P. *Milestones on the Mighty Fraser.* Dent. 1950.

Mason, Ruth. *Torn Between Two Passions.* Self-published. 1986.

McColl, William. *"Report of William McColl, May 16, 1864."* Papers Connected with the Indian Land Question. BC. (Cited by Adams and in *Forging a New Hope.*)

McCombs, Arnold M. and Chittenden, Wilfrid W. *The Fraser Valley Challenge: An Illustrated Account of Logging and Sawmilling in the Fraser Valley.* Treeline. 1990.

Neering, Rosemary. *A Traveller's Guide to Historic British Columbia.* Whitecap. 1993.

Ramsay, Bruce. *Five Corners: The Story of Chilliwack.* Chilliwack Historical Society. 1975.

_____. *History on the Highways.* The Daily Province. Vancouver. 1966.

Reader's Digest / the Canadian Automobile Association. *Heritage of Canada.* 1978.

Riegger, Hal. *The Kettle Valley and Its Railways.* Pacific Fast Mail. Edmonds. 1981.

Sanford, Barrie. *McCulloch's Wonder.* Whitecap. 1981.

_____. *Steel Rails and Iron Men: A Pictorial History of the Kettle Valley Railway.* Whitecap. 1990.

Shewchuk, Murphy. *Fur, Gold and Opals: A Guide to the Thompson River Valleys.* Saanichton: Hancock House. 1975.

Simpson, George. *Part of Dispatch . . .* The Champlain Society for Hudson's Bay Record Society. 1947.

Sto:Lo Heritage Trust. *You Are Asked to Witness.* 1997.

Thomas, Frances. *Golden Moments in the Memory of a Town: Hope, British Columbia, 1929-1979.* Hope. 1979.

Todd, Lewis Paul & Merle Curti. *Rise of the American Nation.* Harcourt, Brace & World, Inc. 1966.

Victoria Weekly Colonist. June, 1858. Cited by Gary Geddes, (ed.) *Skookum Wawa: Writings of the Canadian Northwest.* Oxford. 1975.

Wells, Oliver. *The Chilliwacks and their Neighbours.* Talonbooks. 1987.

_____. *A Vocabulary of Native Words in the Halkomelem Language.* Chilliwack. 1965.

Woodward, Meridith Bain. *Land of Dreams: A History in Photographs of the British Columbia Interior.* Altitude. 1993.

York, Annie (with Richard Daly and Chris Arnett). *They Write Their Dreams on the Rock Forever: Rock Writings in the Stein River Valley of B. C.* Talonbooks. 1993.

History Internet Sites: British Columbia Archives; BC Hydro; BC Parks, Skagit Valley Provincial Park; Canadian Geographic; Cataline's Packtrail; City of Exeter; The Gold Rush Town of Yale; Historic Yale; HopeBC; Hope and District Chamber of Commerce; Hudson's Bay Archives; Kamloops Art Gallery; Province of British Columbia, BC Geographical Names; Seattle City Light; Skagit Environmental Endowment Commission; Skagit River Journal of History & Folklore; Trails BC; Washington State Historical Society.

OTHER (POETRY & SPIRITUAL ECOLOGY) RESOURCES

Banting, Pamela, Editor. *Fresh Tracks: Writing the Western Landscape.* Polestar. 1998.

Berry, Thomas. *The Dream of the Earth.* Sierra. 1988.

Davis, Wade. *Shadows in the Sun: Essays on the Spirit of Place.* Lone Pine. 1992.

_____. *The Clouded Leopard: Travels to Landscapes of Spirit and Desire.* Douglas and McIntyre. 1998.

Dillard, Annie. *For the Time Being.* Viking. 1999.

_____. *The Living.* Harper Collins. 1992.

_____. *Teaching a Stone to Talk: Expeditions and Encounters.* Harper & Row. 1982.

_____. *The Writing Life.* Harper Collins. 1989.

Hope, Lawrence. Telephone interview.

Kerouac, Jack. *The Dharma Bums.* Signet. 1958.

_____. *Desolation Angels.* Riverhead. 1965.

Johnson, E. Pauline. *Flint and Feathers: The Complete Poems.* Hodder and Stoughton. 1931.

Mitchell, John Hanson. *Walking towards Walden: A Pilgrimage in Search of Place.* Addison-Wesley. 1995.

Nihei, John. Personal interview.

Rhenisch, Harold. *Out of the Interior: The Lost Country.* Cacanadadada. 1993.

————. *Tom Thomson's Shack.* New Star. 2000.

Sheldrake, Rupert. *The Rebirth of Nature: The Greening of Science and God.* Park Street Press. 1994.

Snyder, Gary. *The Back Country.* New York: New Directions. 1957/1971.

————. *Mountains and Rivers Without End.* Counterpoint. 1996.

————. *The Old Ways.* City Lights. 1977.

————. *The Practice of the Wild.* North Point. 1990.

————. *Riprap & Cold Mountain Poems.* Grey Fox. 1965.

Stegner, Wallace. *Where the Bluebird Sings to the Lemonade Springs: Living and Writing in the West.* Penguin. 1992.

Swimme, Brian. *The Universe Is a Green Dragon: A Cosmic Creation Story.* Bear & Company. 1984.

Wood, Daniel & Beverley Sinclair. *Western Journeys: Discovering the Secrets of the Land.* Raincoast. 1997.

INDEX

192

CREDITS FOR PUBLISHED WORKS CITED

From M. Bains Woodward's *Land of Dreams* used by permission of Sue Anderson, Altitude Publishing. From Pierre Berton's *The Great Railway Illustrated* and *The Arctic Grail: The Quest for the Northwest Passage and the North Pole 1818-1909,* used by permission of the writer, through his agent Elsa Franklin. From John Clague, by permission of the professor himself. From Wade Davis' *The Clouded Leopard: Travels to Landscapes of Spirit and Desire,* 1998, used by permission of Lisa Nave, Rights Manager, Douglas and McIntyre Publishing Group Ltd. From Gary Snyder's *The Practice of the Wild* and *Riprap & Cold Mountain Poems,* used by permission of Farrar, Straus & Giroux. From Sydney Cannings and Richard Cannings' *The Geology of British Columbia: A Journey Through Time,* 1999, used by permission of Greystone Books, a division of Douglas and McIntyre Publishing Group Ltd. From R. C. Harvey's *Carving the Western Path* used by permission of Rodger Touchie, Heritage House. From Lawrence Hope, used by permission of the Elder himself. From the Kamloops Art Gallery's web site "Onderdonk's Way" used by permission of Roger Boulet and Beverley Clayton, Administrative Assistant, Kamloops Art Gallery. From "The Shooting of Dan McGrew" used by permission of William Krasilovsky, agent for the Robert Service estate. From "The Windchill Factor" used by permission of the poet, Don McKay. From R. G. Harvey's *The Coast Connection* used by permission of Oolichan Books. From *Tom Thomson's Shack* used by permission of the writer, Harold Rhenisch. From Bruce Hutchison's *The Fraser,* used by permission of Matt Williams, Rights Manager, Stoddart Publishers. From Teit, cited in *They Write their Dreams on the Rock Forever,* used by permission of the Seiglers, Talonbooks. From Oliver N. Wells' *The Chilliwacks and Their Neighbors,* used by permission of the Seiglers, Talonbooks.

Quotations from *The Canadian Encyclopedia* used by permission of James H. Marsh, editor, *The Canadian Encyclopedia* © Historica Foundation.

J. M. Bridgeman was born in Rivers and raised on a farm near Oak River, MB. She is a graduate of the University of Manitoba (B.A., Cert. Ed., M.A.). She has published poetry, articles, and book reviews in literary and online magazines. She lives in Hope, BC.